What people are saying about …

Hiding from the Kids in My Prayer Closet

"*Hiding from the Kids in My Prayer Closet*, Jessica Kastner's book about finding grace in motherhood imperfection, gives readers permission to live in the moment. The book embodies the famous quote 'Comparison is the thief of joy.' Instead of focusing on failure, Kastner wants moms to transfer that energy into finding happiness in their own messy, imperfect ways. Even though she might lose track of the school calendar or make dinner from a box, she can still enjoy jumping on the trampoline with her boys or having worship dance parties. Kastner's tales of imperfect, faith-based motherhood will resonate with moms who feel they don't always succeed at 'mothering' but love the path God has put them on anyway."

Angelia White, publisher of
Hope for Women magazine

"Through hilarious retelling of her real-life parenting adventures, Kastner sheds light on the common struggles of raising children and assures readers that God has all of the seemingly impossible messes under control. Kastner's honest and comforting message reminds us that no one is perfect, and God doesn't expect us to be. An inspiring book for all Christian parents doing the best they can!"

Simple Grace magazine

"In this era when we're constantly told to *be* more and *do* more, we need voices like Jessica's to remind us that we can do less and laugh more instead. With humor and truth, she reminds us to lean on God as we navigate the hard parts of motherhood, even when we feel like the job does *not* come naturally!"

Jamie C. Martin, cofounder of SimpleHomeschool.net and author of *Give Your Child the World*

"Loving *Hiding from the Kids in My Prayer Closet*—a super-fun mommy manifesto that's relatable and encouraging. I appreciate Jessica Kastner's way of running all the parenting adventures through a comforting sift of grace. If you ever struggle with feeling you're a less-than-perfect mom (and come on, don't we all?), oh, girl, this book!"

Rhonda Rhea, TV personality and author of twelve books, including *Fix-Her-Upper* and *Turtles in the Road*

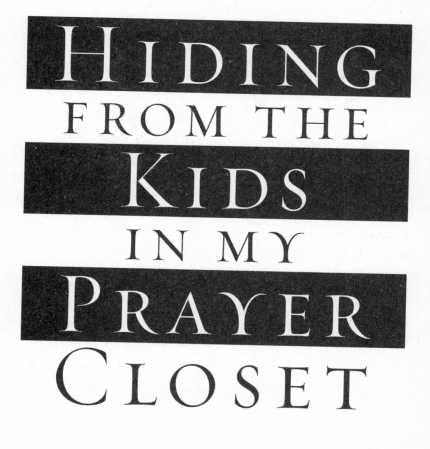

HIDING FROM THE KIDS IN MY PRAYER CLOSET

FINDING GRACE and LAUGHTER WHEN
MOTHERHOOD GETS REAL

JESSICA KASTNER

David C Cook®
transforming lives together

HIDING FROM THE KIDS IN MY PRAYER CLOSET
Published by David C Cook
4050 Lee Vance Drive
Colorado Springs, CO 80918 U.S.A.

David C Cook U.K., Kingsway Communications
Eastbourne, East Sussex BN23 6NT, England

The graphic circle C logo is a registered trademark of David C Cook.

The website addresses recommended throughout this book are offered as a
resource to you. These websites are not intended in any way to be or imply an
endorsement on the part of David C Cook, nor do we vouch for their content.

All Scripture quotations are taken from Holy Bible, NEW INTERNATIONAL
VERSION®, NIV®. Copyright © 1973, 2011 by Biblica, Inc.® Used by permission.
All rights reserved worldwide. NEW INTERNATIONAL VERSION® and
NIV® are registered trademarks of Biblica, Inc. Use of either trademark for the
offering of goods or services requires the prior written consent of Biblica, Inc.

LCCN 2017931373
ISBN 978-0-7814-1484-5
eISBN 978-1-4347-1188-5

Published in association with literary agent Tawny Johnson of D.C. Jacobson &
Associates LLC, an Author Management Company. www.dcjacobson.com.

The Team: Alice Crider, Nicci Hubert, Nick Lee,
Ashley Ward, Jack Campbell, Susan Murdock
Cover Design: Amy Konyndyk
Cover Photo: Getty Images

Printed in the United States of America
First Edition 2017

1 2 3 4 5 6 7 8 9 10

042817

For the three pieces of my heart,
Eli, Kenai, and Jack

CONTENTS

THIS IS WHAT HAPPENS WHEN YOU'VE GIVEN UP PERFECTION

THIS IS WHAT THEY'LL EXPOSE YOU TO

THIS IS WHY WE HAVE 'EM

ENOUGH OF THIS FOOLISHNESS ... BRING ON THE TAKEAWAYS!

Prologue

Motherhood was never going to be the culmination of all my dreams realized. I'm about as maternal as a garden snake and can't even keep a cactus alive. When my sisters would play house, my Barbies were sneaking off to exotic adventures … *The world is ours, Ken.* However, God, in all his wisdom and humor, had a plan. Although I was raised in a Christian home, I fell into a downward spiral of rebellion after my father passed away when I was twelve, turning away from the Lord and pursuing a path of self-indulgence that led to my biggest nightmare at the time: becoming pregnant my senior year in college. I was so engrossed in partying and worldliness (think prodigal son goes to the University of Central Florida) that I saw a baby as the end of all my dreams and ambitions—the end of myself. And thank God it was.

Though I was far from God and undeserving as a person can be, the Lord gave my sister Jill a dream, telling her I was pregnant the day before my abortion appointment, which I never showed up for, after she intervened. I lost "everything" in the process: my friends, my hope, my independence, my pride. And nine months later, I fell in love with a child God used to forever change my cold, stubborn heart, as I really tasted his goodness for the first time.

I raised Jack alone for seven years, as an undomesticated new Christian, sometimes feeling alone and never quite "mommy" enough compared to veteran mom friends who made the Proverbs 31 wife look disheveled. Cleaning interventions were held on my behalf, more than once. This is when I realized I was an "un-mom." I seemed to lack this maternal chromosome beheld by other moms Instagramming their perfect dinners and enthusiastically singing a cappella with strangers during circle time. I eventually married, had two more boys within two years after consistently failing at the rhythm method, and left behind a career to stay home and experience the most challenging, yet rewarding years of my life. God's turned all my priorities upside down, teaching me levels of patience and selflessness I never thought possible and, most of all, to be still and enjoy the path he's led me on.

But although we have the joy of the Lord and a peace that surpasses all understanding, we still face the difficulties and temporary losses of sanity motherhood brings. So this isn't a rosy-colored take on motherhood with continual comparisons to Ruth or Deborah. I choose to laugh at the ridiculous rather than attempt a false sense of perfection that Christian women sometimes fall prey to, or feel hopeless when things "get real." It can be disappointing when our toddler throws cheese at our life-group guests. But I've learned to rely on God, try my best, and enjoy the ride. I wrote most of this in my severely stained bathrobe after 10:00 p.m., when the kids finally stopped begging for juice. I hope it warms the heart of every last un-mom out there. We got this.

THIS IS WHAT HAPPENS WHEN YOU STAY HOME

CHAPTER 1

You Know You're an Un-Mom When ...

Maybe it's because I had my first so young, at twenty-one, but I never had the baby urge. I never lit up or erupted into lullaby around other people's kids. Once I caught a friend smelling a baby's head: "Mmm, it's like heaven!" and I assumed she was a few crayons short of a box. *It's not chicken marsala; it's a human scalp, ya weirdo.* Not an ovary twinge, not a heartstring pulled when holding another's baby. My idea of a "baby fix" was getting whoever's baby I was holding into the grasp of another, ASAP.

With my first pregnancy, Christian relatives tried to assure me that my God-given instincts would kick in:

"You're born for this." *Now that's just insulting.*

"God gave all women the ability to mother—it's just natural." *Gravity's natural. This feels like a night terror.*

One of my sisters, God bless her, reduced herself to bold-faced lying, saying she always thought I'd be a good mother. The same

sister to whom I force-fed screwdrivers at the age of twelve at a vacation bar in Cancun.

I hate stereotypes, and I'm not sure if my resistance to being
categorized as a "mom" stemmed from the fact that I became one
accidentally, three times over, or if I have a slightly negative view
of what society characterizes as a "mom" type. It's mostly all in my
head. It just sounds so unoriginal, like becoming a mom suddenly
embodies your entire personality, and identity—your "you-ness."

Before kids, I was just Jess: a slightly unhinged free spirit, but
whatta dreamer! Then some overachieving sperm decides to go for
glory and that's it: you're a mom. That's who you are. I say this with
the full realization that my kids are my most sacred blessing, but the
problem for the un-mom is the motherhood gene neeeeever quite
takes over. I got into it for a while during pregnancy, ecstatically signing up for BabyCenter.com's daily updates: "Jan. 17th … your baby
is now the size of a chickpea!" *Incredible.* But then I became a mom,
and I patiently waited for that maternal gifting to completely unleash.

But as the years passed, I slowly realized that I was another
breed of mother, and though some might feel the term "un-mom" is
negative, I've wholeheartedly embraced the concept that, although I
might stick out like a sore thumb in many a playgroup setting, I'm no
less devoted to my children. They call me mom, but it will never be
a vanity plate. You'll never hear me chattering enthusiastically about
the next mommy-and-me pottery jam. I don't own scrapbooks. The
thought of homeschooling sends shivers down my spine, and the
closest thing I've done to subscribing to *Parents* magazine is when I
checked off the wrong box, next to *People.* Great. More recycling. I'm
never, ever prepared for the next stage of parenthood, and sometimes

I look at my growing brood of kids suspiciously: Could I really have procreated all these people? Truly amazing. I love my kids more than life, but I've never even attempted to keep up the perfect parent front, and would hands down fail if I tried. And to prove it, I've developed the following list of ways to know whether you are, indeed, like me, an un-mom:

- You've wrapped kids' birthday party presents in Christmas wrap, and on the day of Jesus's birth, vice versa.

- Baby stores give you night terrors, not goose bumps. You'd actually rather jog through a dark alley at night than visit Babies "R" Us, even for a moment.

- You've actually switched churches after hearing about a mandatory signup in the nursery/children's ministry for all parents.

- By the average age of seven, your children began reminding you to sign their homework, turn in permission slips, and gather the lunch money.

- You've missed so many vital school announcements that your friends began a text chain keeping you abreast of weather cancellations, permission-slip deadlines, and professional development days. "FYI, field trip is today."

"What?! OMGee thank you … should they bring lunches?!"

- The bus driver actually yells out "Tomorrow is a half day!!" because you've forgotten so many times. And in pure karmatic retribution, I've stood at the bus stop twice this year, unaware it was a school holiday.

- Your friends pack extra diapers/wipes/snacks when they know you're along for the ride. Basically, they prepare for a playdate with a cast member from *Teen Mom*.

- You'd rather go to a stranger's funeral than arts and craft time at the library. At least you get to dress nice, sit peacefully, and if the moment's right, evangelize to those grieving.

- "Pinterest fails" look like works of art compared to your last four holiday craft attempts. There's a pipe cleaner stuck to a rock on my dresser, and for the life of me, I still can't remember what it was supposed to be.

- When working mothers have commented they could "never" stay at home with their children, as if you were inbred for such a lifestyle, you'd love to reassure that your life's calling is not to read sugar labels and sanitize plastic all day. If you move one more sharp object out of reach, you might actually crack, but this is the selfless lifestyle you've chosen.

- You've been so caught up in daydreaming, dancing around the kitchen, or your work, you've actually forgotten to pick up your kids from a variety of destinations.

- When you managed to send personalized baby announcements to your fifty extended relatives, almost everyone thanked your mother, assuming you couldn't possibly be capable of such strategic planning and execution.

- Your photo Christmas cards have been known to go out past New Year's. Now you order the "Season's Greetings" option, just in case you rinse and repeat next year.

- Other people's children's plays, recitals, or performances of any kind are neither cute nor amusing. Unless it's your kid up there slaughtering a pirouette, you're in a mental prison, all your own.

- You'd rather roll in glass shards than volunteer for your church's annual Vacation Bible School, a weeklong sweat fest requiring you to monitor less committed members' children for three hours a night.

- You've taken out a library card under every one of your children's names because you typically have fines upward of $80. The librarian actually says "Good luck" after you check out.

- Your kids have found their schoolwork or artwork in the trash because you're too lazy or busy to schlepp to the Dumpster in the snow ... and you've lied every time. *"THAT Daddy!"*

- Every time people realize you're a mom, they're all "Oh, really, you have kids?!" You'd like to think it's your svelte figure generating such disbelief, but their faces consistently scream, *This woman's a train wreck. Lord, keep and protect those little ones.*

- In a rare moment of insanity, you volunteered to be your school's "room mother" … It's been a year, and you're still not the same.

Can you relate? Then read on, fellow un-moms.

CHAPTER 2

If This Is How It Starts, It's Gonna Be a Rough Road

Since most of this book deals with parental experiences we never expected, it's only right we begin at the genesis of our maternal journey, where a tiny sliver of our soul was lost, never to return. Yes, yes, this is where we fell in love with our eight-pound manifestation of God's goodness. However the birthing process went, first days of motherhood are often still terrifying beyond measure. And here's why:

It wouldn't have mattered if I had rolled up to that hospital with a doula on one arm and a thirty-page birthing plan on the other, nothing could have prepared me for the crazy that went down in the next forty-eight hours. Experience is the only teacher on this field trip to glory, and trying to explain birth to the layman is like that survivor on the news describing his escape from natural disaster. But here goes.

For the camp of women out there heroically denying meds, I can only assume the gut-wrenching pain is the greatest shock. As a card-carrying member of Team Epidural, however, pain had little to do with my trauma. By baby number three, I could actually detect that sweet metal clanking of the anesthesia cart a full unit away, like Christmas come early. I have a friend who birthed six children naturally, not because she was afraid of side effects, but because she believed it was God's intention for women to feel the pain of child-birth, to bring us closer to him. When she tried to peddle this gypsy logic my way, I was forced to point out that God also condemned men to physical labor in the field, so until her hubs quit his desk job at Microsoft, I'd be numbing my spine 'til the rapture.

I also reassured her that the presence of God would be much nearer when high-fiving the RNs through that last painless push rather than screaming like a Sudanese war chief in squat position. Of course there's excruciating pain leading up to that heavenly needle (who knew about back labor?!), but for me it was the loss of personal dignity that brought the most woe.

For women of modesty, who managed never in four years to change in front of the college roommate or saunter topless through the gym sauna, birthing a child in front of strangers, and the humilia-tion that ensues, is almost too much to bear. I was told the pain would supersede the embarrassment. However, when you're riding the wave of a fresh epidural in total consciousness, and then involuntarily crap yourself in front of a team of professionals, the wounds run deep. I'm not sure what was worse—the public defecation, or the sheer, utter shock felt eight hours later, when being awoken at 3:00 a.m. by a med student rolling me over like a hay bale to check for hemorrhoids. That's right. Unbeknownst to me and all the victims of this after-hours heinie assault, hospitals apparently command frat-boy doppelgangers to do their dirty work past midnight, robbing modest mothers of their last ounce of dignity. *I think, I will die now.*

Coming in at a close second to this twilight delight is the unde-sired slew of visits from the in-laws and family and friends who feel it's appropriate to stop by unannounced, less than eight hours after you've hatched a human and have yet to sleep. I find the tradition of mothers having to entertain a roomful after birth almost as strange and uncomfortable as westernized funeral proceedings. I've never understood the concept of lining up before an open casket and then saying how peaceful the dead look. Same as I still can't comprehend why mothers would want a stream of non-immediates filtering through like tourists at a wax museum, only to perjure themselves and say you look beautiful, and less bloated. *Lying rubberneckers. I look like death. Show's over ... Leave the chocolates.*

I suppose in hindsight, all of the unpleasantry can be seen as a two-day crash course in what motherhood will be like for a year, down to that first time baby cries when you attempt eating, signal-ing your husband's prompt abandonment to the vending machine. Twenty minutes of tense nursing later, zero bites of mediocre pota-toes, and no trace of baby daddy, and there was my baptismal fire to motherhood. Fearing unwanted visitors, rarely sleeping, barely eating, perpetually looking rehab chic, and enduring weak attempts from the hubs to help in any meaningful way. *This is going to be epic.* James 1:2 just got real.

But somehow, even more shocking than the loss of bodily pride and the surge of estrogen-infused emotions and tiredness is the indescribable love you instantly feel for this tiny person. It's just incredible, isn't it? All baby's done is cry and pee, but parts of your heart came alive for the first time. That first little cackle, and that first time their entire hand clenches your pinky. That first long baby yawn, and you're done. God knew exactly what he was doing. For every long, sleepless day that follows is this being that moves your soul like nothing before. Now *this* is someone I'd throw myself in front of a grizzly for. *This* is the kind of love Jesus felt while being sacrificed for us. I'm not sure if I truly realized the depth of God's love for me before having my first child. It's so simple and pure, yet so powerful. Okay, Lord; I get it. But postpartum hemorrhoids? Ugh.

CHAPTER 3

The Mom's Club: A Necessary Evil?

One of the greatest answered prayers in my life was being able to stay home with my two youngest, Eli and Kenai, when they were little. But there is a drastic adjustment that occurs being plucked from the hustle of career life and left alone with verbally challenged beings for eight hours every day. The childless crowd can't really understand. "What's the big deal?" they might say. "You cuddle them, have play-dates, squeeze their little faces all day, right? They *nap*, don't they?" We forgive them because they know not of what they speak. What they don't realize is in between all the butterfly kisses and hair braid-ing lies a seemingly endless parade of tantrums, messes, and sibling wars that make a WWE event look like a peace conference.

And then there's the boredom. This one I wasn't prepared for. It might be a bit taboo to talk about, but the truth is this: sitting on the floor building Duplos with a six-month-old for three hours, especially when you're sleep deprived, can be sheer torture. You do what you can—change up the playlist and inhale the Ethiopian cof-fee grinds leftover from an adoption fund-raiser, but to no avail. The guilt worsens as a Christian when you have the peace surpassing all understanding, *and* the joy of the Lord, but still can't muster up the strength to play Bob the Builder, holding your eyelids up in mental agony. The Lord said he wouldn't give us more than we can handle, but three hours of talking like a demented dump truck seriously tests this theory. But alas, we suck it up, scoop it up, and make Bob proud.

This kind of monotonous pace, when mixed with loneliness, can make us feel borderline crazy. While the kids napped during this season of life, I became best friends with Joyce Meyer thanks to the beauty of DVR. She and I would meet up for lunch together every day at 1:00 p.m. for a dose of encouragement, laughter, and if the hormones were a ragin', a few tears. "Amen, Joyce! Amen ... sniff." This experience, and Daddy's midday phone call, are what we live for.

"How's your day, honey?"

"Well, I almost took a shower, but Eli caught wind of that plan and made sure I stayed put in my own filth. How 'bout you? Tell me something. Anything."

I knew things were really bad when I began commenting about the fluctuating squirrel population in our front yard. Something had to be done.

That's when I noticed the ad. Smack-dab in the middle of my local paper, the possible answer to all my solitary woes. The mom's club. Meets every Tuesday in the First Congregational Church basement. I should've been ecstatic, but I was skeptical. To me, joining a mom's club seemed like pledging a sorority of forced friends, and I could never quite identify myself as being a straight-up *mom*. You know, the kind with those car decals depicting the activity of each family member: mom with grocery bag, dad with briefcase, and kids with soccer balls. If the back of my car had a decal, it would be something like this: dad on a fishing boat, mom praying for alone time, and kids beating each other with Wii remotes. Not my thing. But alas, winter was coming, and my chances of finding a kindred spirit at the park were looking bleak. Surely I would meet me a bosom friend at the mom's club.

So with an open mind and desperate heart, I approached that first encounter with the underground world of the mom's club. I can still see it in slow motion: leerily walking with a baby on each hip down the church stairs, hearing high-pitched mommy laughter and shrieking children. At my arrival, the "leader mom" came from across the room to greet me, and the first red flag was raised. When I was a new Christian, I kind of assumed the fact that we'd all been saved from hell and granted eternal life would be enough to bond us, and make us relatable. Anyone saved for more than a year knows this just ain't the truth. We still have to work to jibe with some of our brothers and sisters in Christ, and this would be no exception.

As I looked around in cold panic, I found myself outnumbered by a twelve-to-two mom-to-"un-mom" ratio. Most everyone was indeed rocking the mom-jeans-and-Crocs look, which I think should be banned in modernized society. One mom was wearing a sweat-shirt with bunnies and names that I could only assume depicted her children. Oh Lord, I know beauty should come from within, but … a bunny sweatshirt? The apostle Peter warned against valuing out-ward adornment, but sometimes it's hard "clicking" with friends who believe barrettes are acceptable hair accessories past the age of twelve.

I could've probably gotten over the outfits if any real conversa-tion had taken place, but 'twasn't so. Just giddy jabber about how old this one was, how drooly that one was. This was expected, to a degree. After all, this was the trench we all shared. I guess the difference is

I use the word *trench* to describe motherhood, and their perspective seems more like a magical meadow.

There was no talk of spiritual revelations or current events, no banter about cool hobbies or even whimsical storytelling of pre-child times gone by. Just teething talk. One wide-eyed outsider with cute boots seemed to be nervously sizing up the scene, but before we could talk, it was circle time, which for those fortunate enough not to know, involves sitting in a circle and singing a capella style with strangers. If the mom club was a sorority, this was the hazing portion. *There's no way I'm singing "Itsy Bitsy Spider" with these culties.*

But there I found myself, sitting cross-legged on a homemade floor mat, wanting to explode in laughter, but mommy to the left was *all* business.

I found myself lip-synching with intensity and wishing I could identify better with the card-carrying, stay-home mom types, who talked about their homemade baby food as if they'd curated the cure to acne.

Of course we all gain some modicum of maternal magic once having kids, and it seems to get easier with time. I have since repented for my judgment of the mom's club, although I still find it hard to identify. I've gone to a few different groups, and shared my woes with Joyce with every failed venture. Needless to say, she understands completely.

The reality is that staying home with your kids can sometimes be deeply lonely and isolating. For many of us, staying home with little ones is the first time we've been alone, without structure, activity, or the continual presence of adults, especially if you're coming from the 9-to-5 world. But I've found this season of motherhood can usher in a new closeness to God, if we let it. When sitting on the carpet with baby for hours, or roaming the yard bent over with my "new walker" for hours, I became more mindful of my thoughts. What am I thinking about this whole time? Are my thoughts filled with gratitude and appreciation of the moment—the fact that I'm even able to be home, my child is healthy, I have a husband who loves me and whom I'll eventually see in six hours? 'Twasn't always so. I began praying and worshipping more during these times, which eventually transformed lots of my loneliness into fulfilling times of intimacy with the Lord.

Being home alone also changed my perspective and appreciation for people I admittedly took for granted, and much to the chagrin of my ego. I don't think I've ever missed my husband as much as that first year home with my second baby, literally counting the seconds 'til that sweet Dodge Ram rounded the corner: *Can it be? … Yes, there's no mistaking the rattle of that muffler; Daddy's home!* Five thirty p.m. was like midnight on New Year's every day at our house. We've got hot, average-tasting food, hugs, and hours of adult convo to catch up on. Have a seat.

CHAPTER 4

That Better Not Be My Reflection

I was in Target the other day, killing time with two babies and justifying a Starbucks purchase, when I caught a glimpse of myself in one of the mirrors. I audibly yelped. Somewhere between changing diapers and wrestling two babies into car seats, I failed to ensure I was presentable for the public eye. The result was me staring at what I wished was a stranger amid merciless fluorescent lighting: mascara smudged under eyes, a baby-carrot-stained scarf, and disheveled hair. I resembled John the Baptist wandering the desert, except he had a good excuse—he was carrying the gospel. I just looked like a homeless waif with a flair for fashion.

As I attempted to smooth my hair and subtly flick carrot off my scarf, I couldn't help but wonder what my sixteen-year-old self would have thought, knowing I would one day leave the house in such a state. Until my firstborn, I was one of those girls who would do her makeup before getting the mail. My biggest fear of marriage wasn't commitment but wondering how I could reapply my eyeliner and look believably natural each morning. I have pictures of my first birth, high on a fresh epidural, fixing my makeup mid-labor. That woman is dead to me now.

For me, vain endeavors were the first and most painful luxuries to die since childbirth. I just don't have the energy, and I usually just don't care. Some moms can keep up the front. I've seen them, sauntering through the park, looking all A. Jolie. I'm more Team Hobo. I'm continually humbled by a friend with six children who greets each day by applying full makeup, slipping into cute jeans, straightening her hair … and staying home all day. To me, there's just not a lot of return on that investment. But dang, she always looks good. I tell her I'm bringin' frumpy back, but who are we kidding. I'm lucky if I brush my teeth before five.

Nowadays, this is the sight my poor husband comes home to, a solid five days a week: me in a severely stained pink bathrobe, no bra, and if he's lucky the hot yoga pants, not the ones from '05 with the sag butt. There aren't enough minutes to shower, let alone blow-dry your hair with two toddlers wreaking havoc in God-knows-what room by then. He says it doesn't matter to him, but one day I had a sweater on and he was all "*Whoa, honey, niiiiice.*" I felt kinda bad. It was the kind of enthusiasm you'd expect from a newly released inmate, not your bathrobe-beaten hubby.

I realize we're reduced to granny panties for a while post-birth, but these sadden me almost as much as mom jeans. No judgment to those flying full-cheeked flag. Just encouraging those standing at the fork between granny and thong. Choose the light, my friends.

I don't encourage over-preoccupation with looks, but I think sometimes women feel that becoming a mom is the price we pay for feeling good about ourselves. I mean terms like "mom arms," or sayings like "She looks great, for having kids!" I'm not sure how the activity of our uteruses correlates to fatty triceps, and I for one think women's curves look even better after having babies. These hips don't lie.

Sometimes we act like becoming nearly asexual is the unavoidable cost of pregnancy and motherhood, but let's fight it! Sure, sex might not be the same post-kid, but you make it work. My husband and I had the rare privilege of living with my mother for a year in between moves, while I was pregnant with my third. Try getting your groove on in the high school bedroom you used to roof-jump from, with an infant in the corner. I could still see the Scotch-taped outline of my Marky Mark poster above the crib. Take that, libido.

Of the many ways having kids transforms your reality, sex hits home pretty hard. If you're used to spontaneity, it rocks your world. Especially if you have more than one. If you're tired come nighttime, your chances at nookie might be reduced to throwing a *Baby Einstein* DVD on and running to the bedroom midday. There remains a special place in our hearts for *Baby Mozart* and all its childlike chimes.

And if you test fate and go for spontaneity while the kids are still awake, may the force be with you. Nothing screams *this is the end of all booty* like your two-year-old busting in on a moment of parental passion.

"Where are your clothes, Mommy?"

"I don't know, honey, but when I find them, they'll never come off again."

Even better is being caught in the throes during naptime and busted by, oh say, your own mother coming home unexpectedly for lunch. Yes, Old Testament, this indeed is why a man shall leave his mother and father and not shack up with your folks.

But who are we kidding? Spontaneous romantic trysts are down to a quarterly occurrence, right along with our I-90 tax submissions. As for the frequency of becoming one flesh, I never, *ever* thought I'd utter the words "I'm too tired." But when you hit thirty, and out comes another kid, sex can feel like one more thing you have to do before bed. I've been reduced to texting rain checks before Daddy even gets home. "Sorry, went to bed … but there's always tomorrow. It's gonna be *hot!*" Unfortunately he took me seriously. *Shoot.*

The good news for new moms is that, eventually, you get your groove back. Baby starts sleeping through the night, and with a little patience and calorie-burning breastfeeding, you feel yourself again. It's amazing how six hours of sleep can respark the romance. The post-baby sexy slump can be a transitional time teaching us to see our bodies as producers of life and not just vessels meant to perform and live up to our Paleo diet's promise. I was so merciless and unforgiving of my body before kids—literally weighing myself daily and complaining when any garb past size 2 felt snug.

Not fitting into the skinny jeans I had packed in my return-home hospital bag under severe delusion taught me a lot about self-worth, despite the frustration. God showed me how much my thought life was consumed by my appearance, and it was pretty grim. I had to retrain the way I viewed myself, my value to my husband, and my priorities. When I was a single mom, I remember rocking Jack in that glider, feeling especially frumpy, and worrying about my appearance to men. I just sat there letting the tears fall, giving over my emotions to God, feeling his powerful, comforting reassurance that I was beautiful in his eyes, no matter what, and

I was worth far more than a small dress size. By focusing on the power of what your body has done—birthing a child—and honoring your body as his temple, it becomes less stressful waiting for your pre-prego body to return. Give yourself a break—our bodies are phenomenal.

CHAPTER 5

The Attached Child: Wrap This

I am the Moby Wrap commercial nobody wants to see. No smiles downward at baby cocooning peacefully while I get stuff done. The picture looks more like a man-child dangling awkwardly from my midriff, narrowly escaping second-degree burns as I boil spaghetti. *Whoa, close call; this kid's got adventure in his bones!* This is the reality for those finding themselves with an attached baby. Either harness your offspring 24/7, or pay the consequences. Before having a kid, there are challenges even the naive idealist expects. I knew there would be poop-encrusted fixtures for a good year. I knew sleep, spontaneous sex, and any word ending in *-icure* would be on the chopping block. I did not, however, anticipate my child would emit torture-grade screams the moment our flesh parted.

To the childless, this might sound touching. How good it must feel to know your baby has such a strong need for you. It is sweet, and it does feel good. For a month, six weeks tops. Any longer than that with another human sleeping on you all night, or demanding your presence within a fifty-yard vicinity, and frankly, you want to go AWOL. This is the moment after making an unwise career choice, when you'd call HR: "Yeaaaa, so I'm not really sure this job is a good fit after all. I think the description of duties was grossly misunderstood. Good luck with the next sucker!" But there is no next sucker. There is only you, alone with a child that hits his own head with inanimate objects if you leave him alone.

So there you are, Googling "child hits head on wall" in the middle of the night, and laying hands on your child to cast out potential demons, after which you army-crawled out of the nursery to avoid detection. Yep, this is your life at night, slithering like a carpet snake, praying your ten-pound prison guard doesn't blow the whistle.

It's at this point you start to panic a bit. You start surveying other moms, asking if they've seen attachment this severe. It's like finding out you have a condition, and you instantly want to know the facts. How long will this last? How can I make it stop? Tell me it gets better! And my queries brought as much comfort as when you Google Image "weird rash." I heard from a woman with a two-year-old who screams every time she leaves the house. Another friend admitted she slept on the floor—in a straight-up sleeping bag—because her kid freaked out ten times a night realizing she wasn't crib side. *Gulp.*

In this season of life with your fifth appendage, you learn to approach life differently. Every spare five minutes without your kid on your hip must be maximized. I can house a Cobb salad in under two minutes, and shower in three. And "alone" time takes on a whole new meaning. If anyone had told me ten years ago that I'd look forward to the dentist with childlike anticipation, I would have cried. But two times a year, it's there, waiting for me in total peace and silence. Yes, there's a man drilling your insides, but it's just you, alone, sifting through *People* in utter, sweet solitude.

I had to pinch myself last year when forced to go to court for an unpaid speeding ticket. A guaranteed three hours of no kids, just me and a book?! Like Christmas come early! This is your life, where court is the new day spa.

Much to my chagrin, reading of any kind is not allowed in the courtroom. What kind of Orwellian society have we become when an overworked mother can't peruse *Glamour* while awaiting her penance?

Sometimes it seems like there really is just no chance for alone time. I used to cherish my nightly jogs, just me and the glorious pavement, until I was gifted with a medieval torture device known as the double running stroller. Really this is just a public display of your poor family planning, on three all-terrain wheels. The double running stroller was my thirtieth birthday present from my husband, complete with an iPod attachment, safety harnesses, and a wristband restraint in case your babies hurl toward traffic after undershooting a curb.

For anyone fortunate enough not to have experienced jogging with this thirty-pound misery craft, it's probably because you've witnessed someone running with such a beast, kids crying for more juice or attempting to claw their way to freedom. The running stroller is an oxymoron that defies everything running was meant to be: freeing, exhilarating, just you and the road. Worries and thoughts clearing out of your mind, as you—"*Moooooooommy, let me ooooout!!!*" Pretty sure I passed an ex-boyfriend on one particularly hellish road run. No doubt he was like *Whoa, missed that train wreck!*

But whether it's a jog, an escape for girls' night, or quality time with a book, Mama *needs* space sometimes. .

In desperate pursuit of such alone time, I've found reasons to leave the house for activities I would have fled from before children. I'm not sure which is worse, the ill-fated Pampered Chef demonstrations or jewelry "parties," where friends talk about a teardrop necklace like it's the world's eighth wonder or you're mocked for asking what a citrus reamer is. Well, I'm no chef, and I'm sure as heck not pampered, but you can sign me up for a $25 turkey rectal thermometer as long as I get to hoard veggie dip for two hours of childless peace.

The most extreme of these escape attempts came in the form of attending a women's "gifting club," which my friend and I slowly realized was an illegal pyramid scheme being investigated by the IRS. That almost didn't stop me. I was so attached to my Wednesday-night snack-a-thons, but the Lord stepped in with discernment, and home I stayed. Just me and my industrial-grade stroller harness.

The good news is more freedom occurs as baby gets older, when they're off the boob and the world is your footstool. It can feel sad at first, retiring that state-of-the-art, duel-action Medela, realizing your baby no longer needs you. Then those three minutes of sorrow pass, and you realize you can stay out past ten without speeding home for the night feeding. (Another blessed maternal truth: some babies won't drink from bottles.) #LordHearMyPrayers.

So there you are, at the Cheesecake Factory with the girls at the sinful hour of 10:30 p.m., making out with the best southwestern egg rolls in the western hemisphere, remembering how easy life can be. Lettuce wraps down, ladies. It's time to party!

This is almost as liberating as that first night out with your spouse post-baby, feeling nothing short of a prison break, running to your car like giddy sixteen-year-olds, seeing a sparkle in each other's eye where the sleepless void used to be. The days of arguing over which trendy place to dine are over, as you lead-foot it to the closest possible restaurant.

"Where should we go?!"

"Does it matter? Anywhere!"

Clearly not grasping the magnitude of the moment, your server assumes you're both high. Oh, the true splendor of sitting childless at Outback Steakhouse, milking your ten-dollar steak for every second of Aussie goodness and praying dessert happens before your mother-in-law calls about the baby screaming. 'Tis better than to have tasted the sweetness of escape than never at all.

Yes, reentering the world after a traumatic infancy offers the greatest of joys. Everything is a thrill: that first day back to the gym, sweating the tears back as you reunite with the thigh chair you abandoned so many months ago. Oh, sweet glute machine, how I've missed your singular burn. However, this time of assimilation has its dangers for the mom recently reentering normal life, as there are certain activities we must resume with moderation after being MIA for a year.

It gets easier when you learn tricks of the trade, like learning to nearly levitate off the bed without detection and using well-honed distraction techniques, but for mothers treasuring their personal space, this is most likely the phase that led to the decision to retire their ovaries.

"Ya know, I think I'm content, honey. How could we love another more than her, right?"

"Are you serious? How could you know you don't want more?!"

"I just pooped with a child on my lap. This family is complete."

Nothing readies you for the physical and mental demands of having severely attached children, but there are a few tips and flip sides to remember after another failed attempt at leaving your one-year-old in the church nursery:

- Well, there's no doubt you're doing a good job. When my child screams as I attempt to pee alone, there are few justifications that make this okay. But trying to focus on the fact that his screams stem from total love helps … a little. I always thought it was a little weird when other people's kids had no problem being left with a stranger, or cry when the babysitter leaves. They're attached because you're their entire world—literally the source of all their security and affection—and no one else will do.

- You now have an undeniable excuse for not attending your mother-in-law's fourth jewelry party this year. Explaining how your child screams for an hour upon and after your departure is a pretty solid reason to pass on yet another obligatory accessory splurge. Same goes for any and all PTO-related events.

- When the kids go off to preschool or kindergarten, you'll be just fine. I used to think I'd be a complete wreck when my kids began school, but after the initial shock, it was fine. I felt like all the years of being with them, twenty-four hours a day, seven days a week, somehow had made it less sad. When our kids are our fifth appendage for years, it definitely lessens the pain when separation occurs. Ya did your time. Time to finally build that website.

- Attachment isn't forever. It's usually a short phase kids grow out of by the time they're three, and those years help form the most important, unshakable bond, whether they remember the moments or not. BUT …

- You have to remember to take care of yourself. I used to feel so guilty if my first cried even for a minute while parting for fifty seconds to run to the mailbox. If you need a break, please take a break! Maybe even call a friend to come help you. I'd put mine somewhere safe, like a crib, if I needed ten minutes to mentally regroup and let God remind me I'm a blessed, blessed woman. *Sigh. Mommy's coming!!!*

CHAPTER 6

From Bebe to Goodwill: Thou Shalt Be Humbled

Some say the way to humility is by asking for it. I say it's by pushing someone through your lady parts and watching the pride diminish. From the time baby is born, we give up so much of ourselves, our past ways and nearly all of our pride, to keep our most precious ones alive, and happy.

Child rearing hit me the hardest in the wallet, as far as pride goes. These little stinkers have stolen our hearts and our bank accounts. It's okay when they're babies, if you embrace the almighty hand-me-downs from benevolent relatives. I'm pretty sure Eli went to school with a cousin's vest circa 2001 this morning. It wasn't until I made the finance-killing decision to send my first to a Christian school that I really got a dose of meagerness.

The burden of tuition has brought me to a level of meekness I never thought possible. I went from crafting my wardrobe from Nordstrom Rack to a little corner of the underworld known as Savers, a used clothing store with zero organization but amazing brand names. Citizen jeans, people. Sure, it smells like bad life choices and the cashier is clearly high on cannabis, but these are the shopping realities you face when raising a family of five in New England.

We've given up Thai takeout, DVR, and all things ending in *-icure* for the sake of kids' karate and ballet lessons. We're told we're better for it, but I'm on the fence. The hair salon offering sparkling water and espresso has long transmuted into a bathroom where my mom cuts my hair with scissors she swears aren't kitchen shears. One time she attempted layers, and I wore a ponytail for a summer.

However, the greatest and most humble abandonment of personal style to date has occurred at the fundamental Baptist school I send my paychecks to. We're nondenominational, not Baptist, but the school was in-town, thus providing busing. *Sold.* This school has no library and no school nurse, and the principal drives the bus, so I'm basically paying for glamorized homeschool. Best part? All the women wear skirts. Period. It's part of their church culture, which I quickly became aware of after earning some jaw-dropping stares escorting my kindergartener through the halls in yoga pants.

At first I fought this oppressive standard. No one's de-pantsing this modern woman. But the self-liberation eventually got old, and I started to feel like the scarlet letter in skinny jeans, especially since I was the only single mom in the school, and possibly school history. So with great abandonment of pride, I purchased the Baptist garb of champions: the denim skirt. Who knew they even kept making this hot piece of apparel past '94? But there it was, gleaming in all its faded-blue goodness, my new calf-length regalia of modesty. I felt like a new woman walking into the school café—*Nothing to see here, people, just a wholesome Christian in some ugly denim.*

My jean embrace was of course just practice for the ultimate of humble surrender: my doleful journey from bikini to tankini. When I was thirteen, all I wanted to do was shed the dreaded one-piece, grow some boobs, and claim the rite of passage into womanhood that is the bikini. So far, one outta two has occurred. Mine was nothing too skimpy or spring breakish, just a nice, classy bandeau top. This can be a polarizing subject in Christian circles, and I totally get it. Not sure we should really be canvassing the coastline in our underwear. Just took me a while to join Team Tankini, which just feels like an asexual body Band-Aid. I am 5'9", with zero curves to speak of, leaving the visual of me in a one-piece quite similar to a prepubescent boy in a wrestling suit. Yeah, yeah, I surrender, Lord. But seriously, an A cup?

I'm sure we'll set foot on the wonderment of J.Crew soil later in life, and beauty treatments will occur elsewhere than a toilet, and we'll be that much more appreciative. I can picture it now, sitting back with a green-tea exfoliate mask, exhaling away traumatic memories such as unknowingly garage-saling at a town councilman's house, whom I attacked in a newspaper column just one week before. I believe the term "nepotistic thugs" was used. The Texas-sized amount of pride I had to swallow was excruciating, as he helped me cram his bouncy horse into my trunk. Humble pie, served up fresh in his $600,000 garage.

Parenthood takes total self-sacrifice, but it always reminds me of Jesus's saying "Whoever loses his life for my sake, will find it." Everything we sacrifice for our kids is totally worth it, as is everything we give up for God. Nothing, not our time, money, or energy, is our own, anyways—it's all his, and anything beyond our gift of salvation is frosting on the cake. I've tapped into so much more of God's heart through having kids. Jesus sacrificed it all for us after walking the earth without a pillow for his head, free time, luxuries, or accomplishing worldly "goals." It certainly puts my complaints in check, when pulling up to Walmart with dread. *ALL things through him who strengthens me ...*

THIS IS WHAT HAPPENS IF YOU ATTEMPT ESCAPE

CHAPTER 7

Planes, Trains, and Somebody Shoot Me

Most parents with very young children will agree that the term "family vacation" is the biggest oxymoron out there. The very purpose of vacation is to relax, de-stress, and have fun. Very little of this occurs on the trip *de familia*, a realization felt before your foot's out the door, after packing half your household items: noisemaker, pack-n-play, room-darkening shades, multiple strollers, and some Benadryl, in case you need to drug your children pre-plane ride.

Parents entering a plane have the same hopefulness upheld on a blind date. It could go well. Or it could be the most catastrophic two hours of your life.

Even if you're lucky enough to score God's gift to airborne parents, the direct flight, it's still like sitting in a tuna can with a rabid squirrel and expecting goodness. There's hair pulling, screaming, physical restraining, and many public health code violations as your kid sits in diarrhea for thirty minutes of turbulence. When the seat-belt signs signal your escape, you find yourself in a ten-square-foot room—just you, six remaining wipes, and a squirming ninja covered in poo. Your victory strut down the runway after that debacle will at least end with a welcome return from your aisle neighbors, who've succumbed to drinking at 11:00 a.m. to dull their senses. Back for another hour of jamming Goldfish in your kid's face and apologizing for every kick to the front seat, assuring yourself that Mickey and all his magic will surely make up for this masochism.

But at least plane rides offer short-term torment. If you take your kids on a prolonged road trip, read the Psalms, do yoga—anything you can to mentally prepare for the eight hours of interstate anguish ahead. The most you've driven is two hours to Boston when the babies were zonked. First-timers set sail for the family road trip with the idealism of a first-time mom heading to the birthing room, armed with a doula and a refusal of the epidural. After the screaming and panic ensue, many of us crack. Those breathing techniques are as good as the *WOW Kids Worship* CD we thought would soothe the minions across state borders. You've sweat through your clothes in a deep panic, realizing maybe we underestimated the gravity of the situation.

And before you know it, usually around hour three, you're reenacting the scene from *Fear and Loathing in Las Vegas*, except you're not Johnny Depp swatting away imaginary flies on a meth-infused road trip to Vegas. You're a sober, sweating mother, trying to subdue a very real, wailing child on your way to Story Land in New Hampshire. Not even shoving a boob in their face does the trick, and the next exit is twenty minutes away. And if you have toddlers near each other in the backseat, the scenario worsens. It's like tethering a Jew and

Palestinian together and hoping for peace. Karma's retribution for my vain refusal of the minivan is me, sitting in the backseat, keeping one from beating the other, for four hours.

Hitting traffic is the only way this scenario gets worse. Sitting still during hour four of the family road trip is worse than getting stuck on your way to work when you have a meeting with your boss at 9:00 a.m. At least then, excuses can be made. But here there is no way out of this traveler's curse. You sit, you breathe, and you long for the next exit.

Good news is all nightmares have an end, and when you arrive at this destination, it's beautiful, for a moment or two. Nothing like planting your feet on the firm pavement at one of the finest three-star timeshares Concord, New Hampshire, has to offer. *Let the fun begin.* But after the bags are unpacked and the bedtime stories are read, it dawns on you. You can barely get them to sleep at home. What on the planet made you think you could re-create such a miraculous event in a foreign room, when you forgot your white noisemaker and room-darkening blinds? I had to fall asleep every night with the two-year-old to ease his panic, while the baby slept with the fan on in the bathroom. We literally peed in the lobby restroom to ensure he slept. All the little necessities you forget about aren't there, like the netted fruit holders and Death Wish coffee always in stock at home.

Everything about vacation, pre-kid, no longer applies. The kids wake up even earlier than normal because they're in a foreign place, making you the one and only guest awaiting the continental breakfast at 6:00 a.m. I spent most mornings on a beach vaca, trolling the sands with baby at sunrise, just me and the seagulls, waiting for the rest of the human race privileged with sleeping to arise. You try to embrace the moment, the beauty and peacefulness, but really, the moment would still be there at 9:00.

And even when we take fun family trips, things can still be *difficult*. Disney can be the most magical place on earth. OR it can be a place where you pay nearly a Benjamin for water-spraying fans after falling under the spell of a persuasive travel agent and a dwindling wallet and flying to Orlando in the summertime. Our extended family of forty decided to experience Disney in a united front one magical mid-July, when the average temperature in Florida is about 95 degrees. I was so hot and dehydrated pushing that stroller, I nearly met Jesus in Tomorrowland.

Similar stress was felt as a single mom when my extended family went on a cruise. It sounded good in theory, except I was the only cousin with a child, thus sitting in a window-less cabin from 8:00 p.m. on, watching thirty relatives do the macarena on the rooftop on the televised cruise station. There's something about sitting alone in a cruise ship cabin watching your mother get her dance on that takes the fun outta the Carnival. Another day I took a wrong turn searching for infant life jackets and walked into a cousin being cheered into his new title of hot body champ.

"Anybody see the baby flo—"

"TAKE IT OFFFFF!!!" *Oh. My dear Lord.*

Being on vacation with small children is like waiting tables on New Year's. Everyone's dancing, cheering, and for a moment, you think you're among the masses, until someone spills a drink and you're back in your place. There's no lounging, or recreating, unless you take turns with your spouse: "Okay, if you watch them while I run to the hot tub, I'll watch them when you go to the athletic club."

Like trading shifts on the night watch. But whether trekking by boat, plane, or car, you try to make the most and enjoy being together for those special times that are truly priceless, living in total denial you'll be returning through the method of lunacy you arrived. *Two more days to live* ...

As strenuous as traveling with little ones can be, I do believe extended time away with the family is necessary, and worth the imminent stress. My dad was a staunch believer in two weeks of family vacation a year, always stressing that we needed to "get away" from normal life in order to really bond. As a full-time pastor and businessman, he wasn't around as much as he'd like, but he always blocked out periods of "quality time" for us, leaving work and ministry behind. And I'm so glad he did, since he passed when we were little, one day after we got back from a Disney vacation. Our most recent memories were of him, wrestling us on the rides and making faces to the camera to playfully frustrate my mom. Vacation time, or even just special times away as a family, is really necessary to help us appreciate and enjoy each other, with no option to work, answer the phone, or worry about daily life. It re-instills the sense and specialness of being a family unit—traversing through theme parks, experiencing cool sites, or making family villages in the sand. You'll probably forget the egregious amount of tolls and interstate traffic, but will most likely remember crab catching with the kids at twilight with not a care in the world. *Honey, did you remember the white noisemaker?*

CHAPTER 8

The Trifecta of Tears

We all know small children can make seemingly normal life experiences a bit more difficult. But I've found three types of necessary outings that bring more than your average level of stress and embarrassment for the new mom.

Exhibit number one: the unforgivably masochistic act of trying to clothes shop with baby or toddler in tow. Years of wisdom have taught me to abandon these attempts altogether, but I waged some good fights before realizing it's almost impossible to buy a swimsuit, a pair of good jeans, or shoes with the fruits of your loins by your side. I don't care how many nonperishables you cram into that diaper bag, there are few women I know who claim victory in this area.

I took my first baby shopping with me when he was nine months old. I was so excited to be even less than my pre-prego weight and was preparing to relish my diminished hips with an impromptu wardrobe update. Now under any rare body-loving moment, pre-baby self would try on half the store inventory, pose in the mirror as if on the beaches of Malibu, and then make the purchase. Attempt this sort of self-indulgent frivolity with a small child, though, and things get real.

I should've known things would be different as I was led down the green mile to the stroller-friendly, handicap-accessible stall. That alone seemed to shadow the glory of the moment. Childless onlookers gawk as you eternally K-turn that beast of a stroller into the "special" stall. What ensued after can only be described as a fifteen-minute WWE event recap in a twenty-square-foot stall. The cube was literally caked in biter biscuit smeared by a screaming infant and littered with many unworn summer tees. I was practically escorted out like a criminal. "Good luck next time, dear!"

And now, having two babies, eighteen months apart, doesn't make it any better. Normally my shopping activities are reduced to playing in the indoor mall playground/bacteria park and slugging down a venti mocha while the boys wreak havoc in toy store aisles. But one day I was feeling extra adventurous and very desperate for a new bra. Looking back, I'm sure it was the latte-infused courage and too much time watching childless women saunter out of Forever 21. It's like they were mocking me, with their relaxed, smug looks and bags of carefully selected apparel.

That was it. I was off to get a very sexy, very padded piece of Victoria's Secret hardware that, darn it, Mommy deserved. Ugh. The only thing worse than the guilt of exposing your innocent toddlers to the fifty-foot photos of borderline porn is getting the young, extra-eager, extra-perky salesgirl who has no idea about the ticking time bomb you just pushed through store borders.

My kids take an average of fifteen to twenty minutes per store before all hell breaks loose, and the clock had started. While childless retailers might think the sight of you knocking into racks with industrial strength might signal a need for assistance, I find the exact opposite to be true. I want to sort through the racks in sheer concentration, with no witnesses to my boys sword fighting with bras on their heads. But no such luck with Brittany, parasitic salesgirl extraordinaire. My attempts to speed stroll to the miracle bra section I call home were immediately thwarted by her need to inform me of every sale under the Pink sun. I wanted to tell her that my nursing children had shriveled my boobs to the size and consistency of African prunes, therefore negating the need for "barely there" brassieres, but I bit the lip.

At least until the fitting room. I don't know at what point I lost control of the scene, but I think it was when one began ramming the door while the other adorned his head with sanitary panty liners. There's just something about fitting rooms that transform my children into bloodthirsty warrior midgets. And of course Brittany and I shared a very intimate moment after Eli pushed the stroller aside, opened the door, and exposed my bare butt for all to see. She completely shut up after that.

This brings us to a less embarrassing, but equally as frustrating venture with children: the doctor's office. It's a petrifying experience from day one, restraining your newborn while he's injected with pain. And it only gets worse when they become old enough to remember the trauma, and consequently kick and scream upon sight of the medical office. You really haven't lived until you've dragged your own child dead weight into a public setting and then waited for a good hour to be seen. And who could blame them? Everything about the experience is awful. On one particularly painful forty-five-minute wait, I mentally drafted a letter to my pediatrician's office and probably would have mailed anonymously if I were PMSing:

Dear overpaid and underserving medical professionals:

Although I appreciate your horrifically flawed attempts at appointment scheduling, I have a few suggestions. While time is clearly a nonissue in your line of work, visitors live in the real world, where we must adhere by something known as the almighty clock. Despite vicious misconceptions that mothers sit around all day waiting for dough to rise, we actually have obligations to fulfill, places to be, and things to do—other than catch a 'tude from a socially inept receptionist. We had to book this appointment six months ago, and the least you can do is get us to examination room #2 before the next decade. Dearest nurse practitioner, please do not roll the eyes or appear confused when I explain my limited vaccination plan and refuse the flu shot. It's bad manners, and if you keep it up, I'll scare you even more by sharing my theories on Extortion 17 and independently generated thoughts on how the FDA is killing us. *Shhh*, don't tell the feds.

"So you haven't vaccinated at all, in the last two years, Mrs. Kastner?"

"Nope."

"Are you planning to catch up with them today?"

"Nope."

"I see." Insert condescension.

Peddle it elsewhere, sister.

So she leaves indignantly, and I'm left at warp level three, waiting for the doctor to red-carpet his way over, while we sit in a sterile room full of things my kids can't touch. I've waited in mile-long porta-potty lines with more patience. One time my two-year-old had a three-hour (THREE!) eye doctor appointment consisting of a full body restraint, while his infant brother filled the room with the stink of poo. Eli's screams through a painless eye dilation were those akin to torture chamber. I left the office in a cold sweat, infant carrier in one hand, toddler on hip.

This leads us to exhibit number three: church. I love church. But the thing about the kind we go to, with long, contemplative worships, is you just want to get lost in the moment. Think about it. How many other experiences during the week give opportunity to dress nice, close your eyes, sing to the music, and thank God for all—"Eli, STOP it, shhhh!" And reflect on life, and all that God has taken you through to this—"STOP SPITTING!" ... You get the point. To me, the misgivings of toddlers and boyish antics seem extra flagrant while gathering with the saints, who apparently all have perfect children. Never hitting each other with Bibles, pulling up your skirt, or barking like a dog during those thirty seconds of silent prayer.

Not to mention my children never allow me to leave them in the nursery, forcing me to stay and play with the children of the apparently more successful parents. I normally try to remain positive during this time, focusing on how my children probably just love me so much more than the rest, but one particular Sunday I just wasn't in the mood. I took Eli back in the sanctuary and let him color or play quietly. We had made it an impressive fifteen minutes before the sweet old ladies behind us apparently smiled too much for his liking. And with that, he yelled, "I'm going to kick your butts!" at the top of his lungs.

I am a solid believer in the power of the written word, but I cannot describe the utter humiliation I felt in those seconds that followed. I escaped our pew like a scene from *The Matrix*, gathering our belongings midair and flying out in seconds. I would've rather bared my buns to the entire Victoria's Secret staff than experienced the horror of that moment.

The good news is, it always gets easier. This is not one of those life coach moments, where your therapist assures life gets better because they see that unstable look in your eye. Everyone's parenting experience is different, of course, but in general, it gets easier. Whether it's because the chronological stages of childhood are naturally easier, or the fact that we're more experienced and confident with each additional child, first-time moms should know that it always gets easier. Claim it, sisters! As sacred and seriously amazing the infant stage is, with all its newness, I found motherhood to become immensely more enjoyable after the kids turned three or four, when our family was able to do things together like play board games and dine out without needing therapy by dessert.

It's like that fog of sleeplessness and fecal fumes suddenly lifts and you're looking at a couple of relatively well-adjusted beings who say thank you to strangers and sit in the backseat without attempting homicidal-grade violence.

"You guys good back there?"

"Yup."

Incredible.

Not to take away from the preciousness of the early years—watching our little peanuts walk and talk is nothing but miraculous—but I view that season as sacrificial, sowing the seeds, doing the hard work, and then reaping the fruit years later. That fruit smells pretty derned sweet when I can bring my kids to T.J. Maxx, purchase a commodity, and leave without crying on the inside.

Baby will sleep more. Siblings will fight less. You will absolutely have time to stand in the bathroom plucking your eyebrows or doing your roots without your eighteen-month-old constantly interrupting and getting an unwelcome dose of ammonia. Yes, there are challenges with every next stage, but you just become more patient, more wise, and more resilient. I wouldn't trade this war-won wisdom and experience for all the laugh lines in the world ... that's what night repair cream is for.

CHAPTER 9

Ode to the Babysitter

When I was a teenager, babysitting was an activity reserved for periods of groundation, or an act of financial desperation. There was nothing worse than being constantly interrupted by other people's kids while raiding the cabinets for the good snacks. So I have great respect for sitters of all kind, showing up on our doorsteps at 7:00 p.m. sharp to emancipate us from our home for three hours of freedom. There is nothing so valuable in the life of a parent than scoring a good babysitter. She's right up there with the trampoline and Netflix Kids.

Granted, it takes a while to find a good one, passing on the goth girl with too many skull accessories for your comfort level, and another who puts the kids to bed in their clothes. It's amazing how the screening decreases over time, as with so many other parental standards we behold with baby number one. One sitter never looked us in the eye, literally communicating through giggles, and another insisted we call her an au pair. After many years of enduring and comparing babysitting debacles with friends, I've developed a pretty solid list of suggestions we dream future sitters would adhere to:

#1. Clean. Up. Your crap. Some of these princesses make more than I did my first job out of college—$15 an hour *per kid* in New

England is reproductive prejudice. Really, she should be detailing my floorboards at this rate of inflation, and yet we've come home to jaw-dropping messes that did not exist before our joyous departure. She'd just be sitting there, knee-deep in a Twitter feud, proudly announcing the kids are asleep, as if we expected them to be sparring at 11:00 p.m. Popcorn asunder, dishes on the counter, and no sign of remorse.

#2. Speaking of media, please for all that is sacred, put down the phone. Aside from the fact that you're overpaid and underworked, our kids met their daily media quota when I shoved them in front of Netflix for an hour to attempt looking human again. I'm not a satisfied customer until you hide-and-seek yourself senseless, endure mind-numbing rounds of Candy Land, and ruin your Hollister threads with craft glue. What were you thinking wearing white? After explaining to a first-time sitter the intricacies of caring for my teething child, the first thing she asked was, "How do you work the remotes?" I made a joke about playing a little game of Amish, but it didn't hit home.

#3. The last-minute cancellation. If you're a parent who doesn't get out much, this is the ultimate babysitting sin. Getting a call from Ugg-a-licious at 4:00 p.m. that she has the sniffles is crushing, whether you were headed to a restaurant or the concert of your dreams. You want to scream into the phone how, at her age, you worked doubles at TGI Friday's on the verge of death, but you refrain from verbal assault.

Instead, you take to social media in momentary loss of sanity, posting desperate messages: "Anyone know a good sitter—need one tonight!" So not only have you broadcast your house will be parentless for the pillaging, but your network of friends knows you're perfectly willing to leave your children with anyone over twelve. If that doesn't work, you take to texting friends, checking on the ages of their teenagers: "So how old IS Jenny now?"

And when all else fails, I've been forced to make the call of dread, to the in-laws, ignoring the feigned enthusiasm and judgmental silence after explaining how the David Crowder Band comes to New England only once a decade. *Just get that Buick over here by seven, Nana.*

Even though I'm lucky to have an enthusiastic grammy and grampy coming my way, it's still a buzzkill. Instead of spending an extra half hour straightening my hair, I'm chiseling crap off the fridge door and trying to find the sinfully ugly afghan they gave me last Christmas. This behavior developed over time, after coming home to find my sister-in-law facedown in my oven, scrubbing away rust chunks, and another time returning to cabinets reorganized and carpets vacuumed by my mother-in-law. What part of this passive-aggressive shaming is acceptable?

#4. The unwarranted phone calls and texts. Please do not contact us for anything but a structure fire, an injury involving a vital organ, or a child missing for more than a solid fifteen minutes. Nothing kills a good time more than your neurotic sitter calling to say the baby's been crying for ten minutes, or your toddler won't eat. She evidently did not read the manuscript-length instructions suggesting ways to calm your eighteen-month-old, and clearly, she's overestimating your dietary standards for dinnertime. A sitter called at 11:00 p.m., two hours after we got to the casino an hour away, to relay the amount of uncontrollable crying coming from the crib. Are there any bleeding orifices? Signs of foul play? No? Then soldier up, and au pair that

keister back into that nursery. But now you face the awkward decision whether to tell your concerned caretaker to suck it up or feign
empathy and let an irrational phobic force you home.

And when it's your own parents calling in a panic, it's even
worse. You're calling before any chance of dessert to tell me Eli's
pink eye looks infected? It's an eye infection. It's infected. There is
a seldom-discussed phenomenon that occurs when your parents
become grandparents, and it's mind-boggling. They're twice as protective and concerned about things that wouldn't have caused an eye
to bat during your own childhood. I'm fairly certain I was illegally
watching my sisters at the age of eleven, but when Nana learned of
my preteen alone for quick errands (okay, for a midday workout),
she nearly fainted. I was mowing my lawn at nine years old, but Jack
landscaping at eleven was near child abuse.

"Um, shall we take a stroll back in time to 1989, Mom?"

"It was a different time."

Well, nowadays 60 percent of grandparents watch the grandkids,
weekly. I'll embrace if you will, Nana.

Babysitting woes lead some parents to give up on the concept
of date nights entirely, but I've never reached that level of desperation. It can be a costly, inconvenient task cleaning the house for
a relative or paying an outsider to man the fort while you catch a
movie, but I think being alone, away from the kids, is vital. There's
something about being out in public, with no distractions, wearing
elastic-free pants, that helps you reconnect and see each other as
your mate, not just the roles of mom/dad or roommate. Even the
best marriages fall prey to the temptation of taking each other for
granted, or not paying much attention to each other, aside from

noticing the pile of plates they left in the sink. Something as simple as appreciating the funny way he interacts with the line of people at the movies, or the childlike excitement he shows discovering his favorite mousse on the menu helps you realize, yep, he's still a keeper. It's worth every last awkward minute driving the sitter home.

"How's school going, Julie?"

"Good."

"Alright." *Twelve minutes to go …*

CHAPTER 10

The Great Outdoors: What Were You Thinking?

"If you want a divorce, take your kids camping." This was my friend's response to my giddy announcement that despite me being nine months pregnant, we were going on a no-frills tent experience sure to bond the fam forever.

Wimp, I thought. My friend was a total princess, and she clearly underestimated my outdoorsmanship. My favorite childhood memories include s'mores by campfire, playing tag in the woods, and falling asleep to the sounds of my dad's guitar playing. Memories I wanted my children to have that summer, despite my water weeks away from bursting.

It took about two hours before realizing that camping itself violates many standards of living we hold dear in normal indoor life. I call them the "three S's": safety, sleep, and sanity.

Let's start with *sleep*. After discovering eighteen-month-old Eli was afraid to enter a tent, let alone sleep in one, we were forced to drive around our campground for thirty minutes at ten miles per hour like predators until he was out. Great until he woke up at 2:00 a.m. crying in sheer, inconsolable panic—and never went back to sleep. No amount of driving, rocking, or begging would do it. He had been duped once, and Mama didn't raise a fool.

All of this would be fine if camping didn't literally suck every ounce of energy from my body during the daytime. From warming bottles over gas-lit flames to terrorizing my kid with freezing shower water, it's really just a perpetual state of disaster.

The next year the youngest two were in diapers, but things looked more promising. I was at least not pregnant, and able to class it up with a plastic cup o' warm pinot while reflecting on the day. Throw in the risk of poison via necking the DEET off each other in spontaneous outdoor passion, and there you have a night of camping splendor. I remember crawling into our sleeping bags thinking the camping gods had smiled upon us, when that life-halting sound of Eli waking up pierced the darkness. Still traumatized by the previous year, Daddy immediately drove him fifty minutes back home to get his four hours of sleep.

On yet another camping extravaganza it seemed we were doing far better. Yes, we had forgotten that we selected a "bring your own fire pit" campground, but we were still happy to sit in the dark and listen to the golden silence of sleeping babies. Just as we were ready to enjoy our warm wine, this time upgraded to tin mugs, our "neighbors" decided to finish their tenth twelve pack and get the party started. My tepid whispers, *"Sleeping kids here,"* only seemed to fuel their insatiable desire to belch loudly and shout profanities all night long. It was then I realized the high rate of campground crimes are not committed by serial killers preying on defenseless tent dwellers. No, no. Such crimes of passion are no doubt committed by sleepless parents at the end of their wits, finally assailing their verbal perpetrators. I had to pray and repent of the anger I felt during that fourth chorus of "Friends in Low Places" at 1:00 a.m.

This leads to the second but no less important "s," *safety*. Aside from the revelation that there's actually no real way to remain clean while experiencing the joy of camp, I realized we had voluntarily placed our children in the exact kind of harm we try to avoid in real life. It took one glance at a bumper sticker on our neighbor's trailer reading "Felons do it better" to realize this. *Why would they put that on if they aren't really felons?* we thought. As if it wasn't hard enough to sleep while envisioning Trailer Joe coming for blood, the sounds of wildlife romping outside our tent literally prompted me to pray for protection all night. And marital disputes are par for the mosquito-laden course:

"Why don't you go over there and tell them to be quiet?!"

"You seriously didn't bring any quarters for the shower? I have to do everything!"

Which leads to *sanity*. Camping takes it away, and it doesn't come back until you return home. While camping, you call into question your marriage, your life, your very state of being.

"Why are we giving our kids marshmallows and chocolate seconds before bedtime? Why does wood burn five times faster than we estimated? Why are we not smart enough to work Jiffy Pop?"

But alas, those moments watching the kids huddled in blankets holding their sticks to the fire and waking up next to their sleeping bag–smooched faces somehow makes it all worth it.

Another place to experience this "joy mixed with pain" is the lovely beach. Ah, the beach. My soul's delight. The heart's true resting place until visiting with small children and watching this sandy post-card turn into a scene from *Survivor* too graphic to air. Beach lovers beware: sweet memories of your single self, lying motionless, sipping green tea with a book will haunt you with every sweltering hour that passes.

Some of my most traumatic moments in motherhood have transpired at the beach. Neurotically lathering SPF 80 on your kids to avoid skin boils, getting half-naked in public trying to beat sand grains off your nipples to breastfeed, and freaking out with every wave that crashes over your toddler. *This could be the one to wash him away!*

During one particularly painful beach day, my friend (with two twin babies and a three-year-old) and I grossly overestimated the time we had to return from our sand bar and the mainland before the tide came in. The water was up to our chests by the time we gathered the garage-load we packed for six kids, causing the panicked crowd of onlookers to quickly form an assembly line to transport our goods and anchor our tubed toddlers. I will never, *ever* forget hearing my friend in a moment of hysteria screaming for her third child … while he was still on her hip.

I know someday when we're old and pruny sittin' on the beach, we'll yearn for the crazy days of old, but until then, backyard pools and sand-free nipples it is.

What I've learned the most through experiences like these is it's worth it to be planful, and come prepared, even for outings as simple as shopping. I used to be the kind of person who ran out of the house for work with heels in hand, forgetting the keys or lunch, or some vital item half the time. This carefree approach is endearing while single. Perfect excuse to eat out. But when you forget to pack a day's worth of snacks, toys, favorite blankies, and distracting activities when venturing out, it can get ugly, fast. I used to laugh at those parents, rolling up to the beach with those eight-wheeler wagons, shade tents, and two tons of toys, until I experienced trying to nap a baby on the beach in July with no equipment. Hard-earned nugget of wisdom, that one.

CHAPTER 11

Wintertime with Kids: So This Is What Prison Is Like

For those of us who detest cold, darkness, and snow, winter can be rough in places like New England. Roaming the house in an asexual Hoodie-Footie (Southerners don't believe us? www.pajamagram.com. Give thanks), driving home at 5:00 p.m. in pitch darkness, risking your life commuting in ice storms, and consistently perjuring yourself when asked if you turned the heat up. *Not all of us have an extra ten pounds of beef jerky–infused body fat, buddy ... Kick it up.* Good times.

But when you have small children, winter woes get a bit more serious. You go from the pre-kid annoyances of chipping ice off the car each morn and selling off stocks to afford heating oil, to realizing you're trapped inside with a baby and toddler for a solid three months, with very few places to go.

There are approximately twelve hours of awake time per day—eight if you luck out with naps—and there are no outdoor escapes like parks, walks, pools, or magical meadows to rescue you from your daily lineup of puzzles, glitter glue, and sibling wars.

"What did you do to make him hit you?!"

"Nothing!"

"Well, if you do it again, that's *it*!"

Repeat that convo at incrementally increasing octaves by the hour and you're desperate to leave the house. These sentiments might sound cynical to the childless crew, but they don't realize that although we love quality time with the kids, eight hours of puppet shows and Candy Land a day make winter a long, hostile purgatory for fun.

The beginning is always okay. Christmas distracts from the impending doom, and lots of new toys and games perpetuate the denial, until about day forty-two of being trapped inside when it's less than 15 degrees out. By mid-January, Play-Doh is dry as dirt, we've failed every Pinterest craft, and we've played hide-and-seek in every corner of this 1,600-square-foot piece of heaven.

Then the snow starts, forcing you to play outside 'til you no longer feel your vitals. Do you want to make a snowman? No. No, you don't. But you do it for your kids, literally counting the seconds 'til you regain blood flow to that last toe. A particularly low moment last winter involved paying my oldest $10 to finish an igloo after I swear time itself stood still. Extra marshmallows when you come in, guys!

Yes, playing outside in winter tests the human spirit, but you haven't truly danced on the dark side of the season until your children take up winter sports. From risking your life ice skating on Aunt Patty's questionably frozen back pond—"Dear Lord, I think I heard a crack!"—to trying to keep your four-year-old alive while sailing down the bunny hill, these joys of winter are in a league of fright all their own. My fondest celebration of winter was perhaps freezing atop a mountain with my child declaring he must pee immediately, while my husband was most definitely warming himself in the waffle hut instead of searching for the hand warmers. I caught a glimpse of our ski passes last summer, and had a physical reaction.

Oh sweet Lord, seventy-three days 'til April.

Suggestions for Winter or Stuck-Indoors Survival:

- The inner-city library is your friend. Most town libraries have kid sections with puzzles, games, and computers, but those within urban areas take it to a whole other level of goodness. The first time I visited a library with actual funding, I stayed for three hours of kid-distracting bliss, while the kids explored puppet theaters, aquariums, and multiple train tables. Truly worth the ten minutes it took to find matching socks for this venture.

- Story time. The sweetest midmorning hour there is for the stay-at-homer. There's no better way to appreciate your tax dollars at work than watching that perky children's librarian entertain the kids with folklore and music for sixty minutes of fun. After discovering this magical gift, my sister and I signed up for every story time slot in all four bordering towns. Even the double header on Tuesdays.

- Museum passes. A worthwhile investment, my friends. Many states allow access to multiple children's museums for one annual fee. Then you won't feel pressure to stay all day to get your money's worth, and you always have a backup activity when feeling especially antsy. "Mom, Kenai broke my Legoooos!!" "Time for the science center, guys."

- Kid swaps. The next best thing to cookie swaps. If you're fortunate enough to have friends with similarly aged kids, arrange one morning or afternoon a week when each watches the other's brood. The kids are entertained with playmates in both circumstances, and you get freedom beyond measure to work, exercise, clean, or stare at a blank wall in pure silence at least once a week.

Some other unorthodox indoor activities I've found to be lifesavers:

- Fill up a huge (like three-by-six-feet) shallow bin with rice, or water, and place a tarp underneath it. This trick got me through a particularly frigid February, with the kids entertaining themselves for hours playing with their mini figures and other small toys in the rice or water.

- Duct-tape large sheets of art paper to tile or wood floor and let the kids go wild with markers, crayons, stickers, and craft supplies.

- Find silly kids dance videos like *Going on a Bear Hunt* on YouTube, or find "brain break" websites, such as gonoodle.com, used by elementary schools and have dance party until naptime beckons. We usually don't even need videos—just put the Bethel Kids Worship station on Pandora, and we're jammin'.

- Make use of the hundreds of dollars' worth of destroyed Legos now piled in knee-high Tupperware bins, and hold occasional Lego-building competitions, challenging your little craftsmen to make the most unique creation for a reward. No one's beneath bribery during these desperate times.

THIS IS WHAT HAPPENS WHEN THEY OUTGROW THEIR PULL-UPS

CHAPTER 12

Daddy's Watching You Today, and Other Lies We Tell Ourselves

It took approximately three hours for me to be out of the house for a women's retreat before my husband lost our two-year-old. He chased the dog out the back door, ran three backyards away, and was gone fifteen minutes before Daddy found him. He was full commando with only a shirt on, of course.

Before kids, I never thought my current reality could be possible. I wish I still clung to the idea that my children's safety wouldn't be compromised the second I left home. But life is the greatest teacher, and now when I leave my babies for an elapsed amount of time, I write instructions more detailed than a senate bill, check in every three hours, and have my sister on 24/7 standby. Insurance cards are taped to Daddy's steering wheel.

I never paid much tribute to gender differences until I was married with kids. After living single through my twenties, it was an atmospheric shift having help. Who knew someone could rewire a basement, change brakes, and shovel the driveway in an hour flat? However, much to my chagrin, these Herculean feats stopped short of the baby department. Asking this man to change a diaper or, heaven forbid, bathe an infant, was pointless. He perfected the art of disappearance every time the baby cried or smelled, and I swear he pretends not to hear crying past midnight. He spends so much time in the garage, our kids check there first when they can't find him. "Check the shed. If he's not there, honey, he's probably rechopping wood to avoid helping Mommy!"

This behavior is all good (not really) until Mommy tests fate and leaves home for more than a day. I'll never forget the fear in my bones kissing my babies good-bye for three days to visit my sister in Kansas City. "Okay, Mommy loves you. Let me look at you, and this house, one more time and remember what was." The worry subsides a little when you get to sleep past seven, eat hot food, and straighten your hair for the first time in nine months. You forget how simple, how *easy*, life was before kids. Want to go out for lunch? *Pinch me!* Midday movie? *They still have those?!* Want to stare in the mirror for ten minutes reshaping your eyebrows? *Heaven has found me!* But you pay the price.

Returning to the house on Daddy's watch after forty-eight hours is like that postapocalyptic return on *The Walking Dead*. Shrapnel of McDonald's and pizza boxes asunder. Sheets off the beds, toothbrushes bone dry, and kids returning from a public outing in each other's clothes. It's bad for everyone. There should be some universal handstamp signifying to the world when Daddy's on the clock.

"Forgive all high waters, cheek crust, and Einstein hair. Daddy has mastered the stock market but apparently cannot maneuver a comb."

And although he means well, the differences between Mommy's and Daddy's qualities of care become even more flagrant when, once a year without fail, our house falls into myriad sicknesses beyond measure, taking hold of one family member, then another, until they plummet into a domino line of puking, fever, and occasional hallucination for a week straight.

It starts with one kid's piercing scream at about 1:00 a.m., hurling dino-nugget chunks in their bed, and it doesn't end until everyone gets taken down. Soon my living room is transformed into WWII hospice—blankets, sweat cloths, bedpans scattered about— and me, the heroic but slightly less ravishing nurse, trolling through the bodies offering water and comfort to all who receive.

Oh, the horror. I sit there, in my own undeniable stench, wondering if there's been a longer week in human history. I daydream of driving my car, fantasize about the taste of coffee, and try to remember what it was like sleeping without the exposure of human waste. The only thing worse than my children's perpetual hawking and hurling is what lurks from my bedroom, where the biggest woe-befallen child, Daddy, ails in flu-like self-pity. There is nothing, nothing I say, worse than a sick man. Another stellar realization achieved when married with kids.

The same superpower that enables women to suffer through pregnancy and birth pain comes into play during these times of woe. I would stand before a congressional jury and attest that my husband would leave our kids lying in a pool of their own waste before doing anything while sick. I've often slithered into our room, sick as a dog, and peered at him, questioning the brand of lunacy that led me to marry this abandoner. *Death do us part my butt. This guy would leave me for an aspirin.*

Being sick while still having to care for a whole family is rough, but even during the lowest fever-soaring moments, I think how seriously blessed we are that these sicknesses are fleeting, and not permanent. I've only had to take my kids to the hospital for minor injuries, like slamming the car door on Kenai's thumb (not an Instagram moment), and I'm always silently moved to tears walking by the rooms of the children living with serious illnesses. Just picturing what it would be like watching your child struggle and endure pain and sickness is almost unbearable. Aside from my salvation, the single greatest blessing in my life is the health of my kids. In a world with so much suffering, it's something I never, ever want to take for granted, and it really puts those sickness debacles into perspective. Once after forgetting to include "and heal all the sick people" in our prayers, Eli solemnly pulled me aside: "Mom, I still prayed for the sick people in my head. That still worked, right?"

"I think so, honey … But we'll keep praying, just to be sure."

CHAPTER 13

Thongs and Barney Songs

As Christians, we're always conscious of the fact that we're "outsiders" in the world, as morality seems to decay and our surroundings appear more end times by the second. I thought for sure Jesus was coming back last year when Bruce Jenner won an ESPY award for courage.

I find this heightened awareness of sinking cultural standards increases tenfold after having a child. You take one look around and think, *Heck no am I raising my baby in this nonsense.* Many mom friends have shared similar fantasies of taking their family, colonizing an island, and never looking back. On this island, the following would be banned: Bratz dolls, MTV, thongs for ten-year-olds, the Kardashians (just because), and dance recitals with six-year-olds shaking their stuff like Vegas showgirls.

It's clear to me now that I was never meant to have girls. I'm continually horrified at attacks on childhood purity by the oversexualization of, well, everything. From *How to Train Your Dragon* characters hurling lewd comments at each other to nasty Lady Gaga songs being played at the children's fun center, childhood innocence is being increasingly robbed.

You can't take your kid to the movies without someone bust-ing out in a twerk, or stomaching the one f-bomb the MPAA so graciously deems appropriate in a PG-13 flick. Something about hearing "Nasty Girl" at 72 decibels while riding the Tilt-a-Whirl takes the fun out of family time.

And if you're daring enough to follow the news, the world is even more terrifying for the new mom, with potential child preda-tors or school shooters lurking around every corner. Or Miley Cyrus gyrating next to some innocent. And there's only so much you can do. Cyrus is an easy one to explain—I tell my nieces that mental illness makes people dance in their underwear—but that's all I got.

Maybe I'm sensitive because we Generation Xers had an actual childhood. I played My Little Ponies 'til the seventh grade and idol-ized Paula Abdul, who exudes monastery-grade modesty compared to today's teenage heroes. I digress. There were no Bratz dolls mim-icking meth addicts or padded training bras back in the day. If we wanted such things, we had to use our good ole imaginations and stuff our bras with Kleenex. I woulda probably sold a sister for a padded bra back then, but I'm glad I was spared growing up in a time when you were expected to have cleavage at twelve. Please.

As my kids get older, I find almost everything the world deems kid-friendly to be inappropriate. My son's *Clash of Clans* computer game seemed innocent enough, 'til I noticed pop-up ads with cartoon clan girls that would make a sailor blush. Just when you thought you were safe: animated hookers, cavorting around every app.

Years ago, I went on assignment for a news story about the increase of scantily clad high schoolers. I might as well have been covering the bust of a Ukrainian prostitution ring. Girls with half shirts, more makeup than a MAC salesperson, and hallways lined with glitter and push-up bras. I felt sorry for them, irritated at the parents, and glad I had sons. Best quote of the piece was from a girl in fishnets and Daisy Dukes who disapproved of the school's plan for a stricter dress code: "Like, I totally think it goes against our right to express ourselves and be who we are, ya know?" Her boyfriend totally agreed.

I know the swift degradation of anything good is inevitable these days, and it's our chance to shine more brightly, but it's still scary raising kids in what can feel like the new Gomorrah, with downloadable porn. For us, it comes down to trusting God and instituting Pentagon-worthy parental controls on every tablet, computer, and phone under our prude ole roofs. Maybe even the digitized coffeemaker.

The truth is, motherhood forces us to trust the Lord in ways we'd never thought possible. Really, did we even know what it was like to truly worry before having kids? I find whatever stage of motherhood I'm ushered into, there's almost more and more reason to worry. I'm actually shocked we aren't all gray as squirrels by forty.

It starts from the second they're born. Your biggest concern goes from wondering how you're going to consolidate credit card debt to worrying whether your baby has stopped breathing because he slept for longer than three hours. You never see this scene on Bun in the Oven's podcast. Literally waking up out of a dead sleep at 5:00 a.m. and sprinting down the hall to see if your child is still living. This. Is. Crazytown. Flash forward twelve months and the gruesome horror perpetuates as you worry about your kid crawling through minefields of potential choking hazards and suffocating to his death, by the hour. I ask you, what other life experience leaves you continually questioning whether a human in your care has been kidnapped, ceased breathing, or nearly run over by cars because you took two seconds too long closing the trunk?

There are so many different kinds of things to obsess over when you become a mother, and it never goes away. When teetering on the verge of a nervous breakdown somewhere between my six-month-old's collision with a car door and an unfortunate battery ingestion, a "mother in the Lord" pulled me aside and did me a solid. She said, "You know, you gotta realize God loves your kids even more than you do." Huh.

At some point in our lives, we've recited and most likely have had some sort of Proverbs 3:5 signage in gold calligraphy hanging on our walls: "Trust in the Lord with all your heart." Then you have kids and this creed translates to "*Help*, Lord!" Because having kids is like living with your heart outside your body, vulnerable to the world's influences and temptations and endless germs. Having children absolutely forces you to trust God in ways you never imagined. Hey, control freaks, guess what? You have zero control. Germophobes, I've got news! Your kids will roam in a cesspool of viral matter while in any kind of day care, church nursery, or kids' play area. Neurotic overprotector, here's one for you! You've just birthed children into a world that some theologians believe is in the end times. Fasten your seat belt.

We now depend on God for so much more than our own good. We have to believe he cares about our kids' protection, health, future, and salvation even more than we do. This is our chance to trust God; I mean really trust God. Our kids are his gift to us.

He knows what he's doing. For some reason it is so much easier to follow Philippians 4:6's teaching to pray about everything instead of worrying when it comes to your finances, friendships, marriage, and work struggles.

But not losing your mind the first day your strategically sheltered teen enters public high school? That takes some faith. I felt like I was watching Jack walk through the gates of hell that first day, white-knuckling my steering wheel and questioning how I could send him into a spiritual vipers' nest at the age of fifteen. It's the hardest to pray and trust God when it comes to our deepest maternal fears. For me, that fear was wondering if ten years of Baptist schooling, where Marvel Comics T-shirts were considered devil's garb, had given Jack the worldly common sense of an Amish farmhand, thus making him vulnerable to the wiles of some sexually ambiguous goth girl within two days.

But alas. God is bigger than our sometimes-shameless lack of faith. We've raised our kids in the knowledge of Christ and saturated them in the presence of the Holy Spirit their whole lives. God is faithful, not only to our prayers, but also to our kids, who belong to him alone. They'll trip and fall, but we need to realize if God can take our own screwy hardships and difficult seasons (oh, sweet Moses, the college years) and turn them into rainbows, or at least some semblance of unmedicated normalcy, he can do the same for our kids.

The problem is we get so trapped in the difficulties and fears of the moment, the big picture becomes blurry and we lose faith. Your ten-year-old might be showing signs of suppressed anger and irregular solitude, but he'll most likely not be a sociopath by the age of twenty-one. Think about some of the struggles, bad ruts, and phases in childhood—and if we're honest, even adulthood as Christians—that God has pulled us through. Physically, spiritually, and emotionally. He'll be no less faithful for our children. Entrust every minute of their lives to God, forgive yourself for the occasional freak-out, and remember, God's love trumps ours.

CHAPTER 14

Batteries: The Other Gold

Most parents agree we're fortunate to live in the golden age of technology. Baby video monitors, car DVD players, Netflix Kids—all treasures to the mom's soul. How those colonial mothers manually expressed milk and lived without white noisemakers is like the eighth wonder of the world.

However, anyone with kids past two has been exposed to the other side—the *dark* side of technology. It's a grim dance with madness. It begins with that first titanic meltdown when the Wii game freezes, or the Nintendo DS charger is lost. You're left helpless with game-addicted children who need their next fix, fast. Oh, the tantrums, the fits of madness that have ensued because of technological error. You try your best to remedy the situation, but deep down you know no amount of rubbing the disks on your boob or scraping crud out of the DS will do it. That scratched disk is now joining the graveyard of chewed and scratched games that collectively cost more than your car, and suggesting we "unplug" and do a craft only heightens the outrage.

It's during these times you realize you've created monsters. Entertainment-dependent monsters who lose their minds when told to pause Super Smash Bros. before the level is complete. I never thought I'd become this mother, coming home to find one kid on a tablet, one on the Xbox, and the other glued to Minecraft. "Hi, guys!" Silence.

The truth is, technology just creeps into your family. And you let it—half for convenience, half because of guilt. For us, it all started in elementary school, with the handheld wonder called the DS. One by one, all my kids' friends came to school with them, increasing the pressure until I was faced with eyes sadder than a World Vision ad.

"Mom, James and Luke both have a DS!"

Makes sense. They've always been spoiled.

But guess who gets a DS six months later? My seven-year-old-turned-federal-lobbyist after browbeating me with guilt and manipulation. I told myself I'd simply limit them: "No playing in bed, and only thirty minutes a day!" But it's easier said than done. Either my husband forgets to monitor them on his watch, they sneak it onto the bus, or wherever, or I decrease surveillance simply because I'm too busy or exhausted. And so it begins.

Before long, my kids became more computer proficient than the both of us and the home office was commandeered by Lego.com, Webkinz, and Minecraft. One night Kenai actually sneaked out of his bed at midnight, downloaded Google Chrome, and installed a PBS Kids game. He was three and a half. It's actually a bit scary. And forget about keeping track of their screen names and login info. You haven't reached full parental shame until you've thrown an adult tantrum while bent over your keyboard in a struggle to remember which email account you stored your kid's Club Penguin password on.

"Oh, forget it, this password isn't working, guys."

"Mom, my penguin name is Mr.Cuddles28 with *no space* between the words, *remember*?!"

It's maddening. I've actually called my bank suspecting fraudulent activity after noticing a $7.99 charge from Ohio. Online embezzlement? Identity theft? Nope, just my kindergartener linking Google Play to my credit card. I don't know which was more disturbing—the fact that he unknowingly hacked into my bank account, or that online penguin-hood costs eight bucks a month. *Mr.Cuddles28, your time is up.*

I'm glad my kids are riding the wave of the future, but it's a little scary when they progress beyond my skill level and I'm useless when they need help. I've written a thesis in a day; how could I not know how to get Minecraft on creative mode? Alas, I'm over twenty-five and thus powerless in the land of Super Sonic and Lego Batman. "I don't know, guys. Mommy can't get this to work. I'll make the good macaroni to make up for it."

Perhaps the most helpless technological battle yet was having to reinstall Jack's Xbox after moving. Can all owners of this black box of woe just unite and propose a national holiday for the earthly saints known as the Xbox live support team? After two hours of reconfiguration failure, I was teetering on insanity. It was 11:00 p.m. on a Friday night, and my voice-crackling thirteen-year-old was one crossed wire away from me belting his bottom. "MOM, we already tried changing the host name! UGHGH!!!!"

It was with utmost desperation that I called live support (located on the West Coast, three hours behind EST, praise 'em!). What I got on the other end of the phone was "Meg," a nineteen-year-old cyber genius, who within minutes, remoted into our computer, did something questionably illegal, and even suggested a lower data-storage plan to save money. I had nearly busted a varicose vein trying the exact same procedure, and she mentally dwarfed me in minutes. I told her I was sending virtual hugs and assured her she would take over the world someday, which in hindsight, might have been overkill.

After enduring traumas like an Xbox malfunction—the sweat has dried, and your blood pressure stabilized—you find yourself daydreaming about a simpler life. A life without gaming systems and smartphones, and a family who remains stable even when the batteries run out. You can only take hearing "Mom, PLEASE go get some batteries!" for so long before surrendering and driving through snow squalls for the copper top we serve.

Battery juice and Lego plastic: the fiber of our lives. Every woman with a kid past five can attribute at least one gray hair to the stress felt searching for that lost stinking Lego piece, or intercepting sibling wars after one busts up the other's set. The word *tantrum* simply cannot relay the loss of emotional control that occurs with just one smashed Lego ship. After accidentally stepping on a Lego craft once, I frantically reconstructed that thing like my life depended on it. *Oh no, they're coming ... WHERE does this piece go?!* Practical note: Lego instructions for every set can be found online. Bless the World Wide Web.

Reconstruction Lego carnage is nothing, however, compared to the painstaking effort it takes building a brand-new set. As a single mom, I felt dread in my soul when Jack got Legos of any kind. Hours and hours of my life building the smallest of sets. "Mooooom, are you done yet??" I actually stayed with a boyfriend through Christmas because I didn't want to build the Star Wars AT-AT walker alone. *Sorry, dude, it's one thousand pieces.*

And even when they grow up and build their own Legos, something in toy hell always goes wrong. How wrong, would-be parents might ask? Take this past Christmas when I skimped on groceries for a month to surprise my oldest with an Xbox One. All was festive until we realized this overpriced gaming system requires an HDMI TV, which is different from a flat screen, unbeknownst to me. No stores were open, so he spent Jesus's birthday sadly staring at a blank screen until a friend showed up with an extra TV. But this was not the end of our tech woes. Apparently there was a national hacking attack on Xbox's server that day, which interrupted all gaming. It was on the news, but since we don't watch TV on Christmas, we assumed ours was flawed. For anyone yet to experience the irrational moodiness of a pubescent teen, count yourself blessed.

Xbox and online fails aside, technology does have its sweet side. The use of handheld devices and downloadable iPhone kids apps have saved all moms from ensuing meltdowns in places like restaurants, visits to the Department of Motor Vehicles, and unexpected traffic jams. After missing our 7:00 a.m. flight from Disney back to Connecticut this year, I have never been so thankful for the existence of electrical outlets and complimentary Wi-Fi. There we were, all tethered to our respective plugs with laptop, tablet, and phones, probably looking like the worst example of familial tech addiction, but not a whine or a "When's the airplane coming?" from the kids the whole time. Judge away, people.

It can be difficult tracking and restricting the kids' time on their tablets and making sure all our devices are on safe mode, but technology helps a lot with parenting too. The most obvious would be the glorious beauty of the search engine, especially during homework time. I have Googled my way through platypus reports, answers to science questions, math formulas, and on and on. Do any of us remember the formula for pi when our sixth grader asks for help? Hmmm … where's that phone …

Some forms of technology like cell phones and even social media can even help us connect more with our kids, especially as they get older. Two words: Tracking. App. Thank God I don't have reason to use it, but it's nice to know that if Jack says he's at the amusement park 'til 11:00, there's highly developed software to prove it. Texting a quick check-in with Jack when he's off with friends or activities— "Make sure you shower before you leave!"—helps when things get busy and usually keeps the neurosis in check. We've gone so far as to become Instagram friends, which he seemed to tolerate until incriminating himself by "hearting" my photo … at 1:30 a.m. "Jack, I know you're awake up there. Get *off* the phone!"

CHAPTER 15

Raising a Teen: Because God Has a Sense of Humor

We all know that nothing prepares you for having babies. No words can do it. You just forge your own survival path. I find the same to be true when your baby somehow turns teen, despite your efforts to cement him into the fourth grade. Nothing braces you for that first time you notice that hint of man-shoulder, or you realize they're walking slowly in the mall because they're shamed by your mere presence. Oh, the cruel world that awaits the nostalgic mother finding herself with a teen before she's ready.

One of the biggest challenges in raising a teen can be finding ways to bond, especially in father-daughter or mother-son relationships. When they're little, it's easy. I've spent years of my life sword fighting, Lego building, and bug hunting. But then at around ten, if you have a boy, an inevitable curse called Xbox happens, and you're done. Your former buddy gets a headset and a few gamer friends, and your interaction is reduced to providing meals and supplying batteries for the remote. So you're left with a decision. Be replaced by cyber friends, or become one.

I lasted a week. To this day I question whether I have a handicap that surfaces only through playing *Call of Duty*, or if I'm just mentally handicapped. I had a better chance piloting an actual plane than getting through level one.

"MOM, you're going backward … Mom, you're shooting YOURSELF!"

Since this plan was a clear fail, I became hopeful when Jack asked to start watching PG-13 action/sci-fi movies and agreed to let me join.

I had no idea what I was in for. Since I was raised in a houseful of women after the age of twelve, the closest thing I came to watching violence or action was Mr. T.—and that was only to fuel a perplexing obsession with an *A-Team* member. Never saw *Goonies* or *Gremlins*, and I thought *Rocky* was a documentary until recently. So after watching the first few of these quality flicks, I made a scientific discovery: time can stand completely still by watching a seemingly never-ending action flick. Unfortunately something about them makes me want to instantly fall asleep, or club myself unconscious. Just when I think we've seen them all, Jack discovers some old version of *Spider-Man* or they come out with some awful *X-Men* sequel. Around every corner lurks a *Mission Impossible*, since 1996, *Ghost Rider* (literally a Harley-driving dead man with a perpetually flaming head), or Lord of the Rings trilogy that hijacks eleven hours of your life. Seventeen hours, if you include the Hobbit movies. My wounds are too fresh to discuss Star Wars, as I would rather eat grass than sit through one more second with Jabba the Hut. *What kind of laced ganja was Lucas smoking?*

So this is my reality when I hear those words, like a slow-motion defense siren signaling disaster: "Mooooom, ddoooooo youuuuu waaaaant to waaatch a moooooovie toniiiiight?"

It's gut-wrenchingly awful but always worth it. Because for two hours of bad acting, corny jokes, and irreverent violence, he will sit in my presence and even share a blanket with his phone off and his thumbs at rest.

The smartphone, purchased during a momentary lapse of sanity last year, also poses quite a challenge for parents of teens. The problem isn't so much that he's glued to it day and night. I set limits. My dilemma is that the time it requires snooping through the darn thing. Anyone judging the habit of spying on your kids, just wait. Wait 'til Molly McBooberson starts hanging on your kid, yelling, "Text me, Jack!" across the school parking lot. We'll see where your integrity lies. *We have a no-dating rule in our house, chicky. Back it up.*

Problem is, after you hack in to their texts, you can't decipher what on God's earth these kids are saying. It's all cryptic, and everything's an abbreviation. What the heck does "GLHF Jack" stand for?! *Dirty temptress, wait 'til I Google this.* As it turns out, GLHF stands for "Good luck, have fun." I quickly repented, but there are many unresolved text exchanges I've yet to decode. A sample of an actual text:

Jack: "IDR if u want a 121"

Flirtatious girl: "Haha OMG ur funny!"

Jack: "JJ that's what he said to Jen"

Flirtatious girl: "404 if that's why she was 555"

Jack: "haha she thinks of him AAF"

Flirtatious girl: "Gotta go 88!"

Crack that da Vinci code of nonsense. I find the whole hormone/opposite sex issue to be the most challenging of it all. My discussion with Jack about how we don't believe in dating until maturity could have won records for awkwardness, concluding with me mumbling something about purity and tossing *I Kissed Dating Goodbye* on his bed. You just want them to remain pure and innocent and stay your baby for, like, ever … or at least until you can figure out how to properly snoop.

Indeed there's some confusing parts of navigating through teen-agehood. Suddenly there's an overly dramatic man with face fuzz in your house, who wanes in and out of childhood based on his mood. Like a hormonal gremlin. And you never know which side you're gonna get. Your happy, well-adjusted teen might emerge from his bedroom, sweet as can be, or you could get the pirate on steroids: "Mom, where's my hair gel?! Arrrrggg!" One second he'll be sitting cross-legged playing Transformers with his brothers, and the next he'll accuse you of being "*so* eighties" (the teenage term for anything uncool—he has a point).

As Christian parents, it's hard not to panic at the first sign of rebellion, or youthful waywardness. The first time catching him tex-ting past midnight, I practically questioned the poor kid's salvation. I've realized early on that having a teen is God's way of forcing us to trust him in ways we never thought possible. We're so used to pro-tecting our kids from the world, it feels nearly impossible to loosen our grips and let them navigate their way through it. I suppose the occasional attitude and head-butting should to be expected; even the godliest of families face their challenges raising a teen.

However, what I'll never accept is the most offensive of all teen habits: the ill-fated eye roll. It took one time for Jack to realize his mother would bring more than the eighties if such a mistake reoccurred. Something about the eye roll, or the snotty "OKAY, Mom!" ignites a wrath beyond measure—I still can't explain it. All the memories of slaving through science projects and sacrificing hair appointments to pay for karate come flooding to my mind … *I've worn smelly, fake UGGs for this punk*. And then the outburst occurs.

"If you think I'm going to put up with that look on your face, when I've given you everything …" I might have brought starving children in Africa into it. But my methods are nevertheless effective. His room might disgust, his feet might reek, but his eyes? His eyes doth not roll.

CHAPTER 16

Science Projects, Fifth-Grade Math, and Other Reasons the Childless Should Celebrate

It wasn't until my kids entered school that my inner anarchist came out. For one, I don't even believe in homework. The Chinese are winning, people. The jig is up. Kids should be able to accomplish their work in the seven hours they're away from home—not trucking a tree's worth of work home every night. Some kind of atmospheric shift has taken place between the time I left school and became a mom, and it's not good.

It's just so *involved* now. Each kid has to log in to learning sites for "e-practice," you have to sign every assignment like a congressional bill, and teachers constantly email updates, reminders, and requests. An actual email header: "Reminder: Dress like a President Day is Tomorrow: 100 percent Participation Encouraged!" Okay, that one gave me enough time to prepare and avoid taping cotton balls to Eli's face, but the prior ten were unnecessary.

The most egregious to date is an email from my son's fifth-grade teacher, worrying that Jack was running behind on his research for a project ... due in three weeks. There were two versions to my response that day, and the unsent message might have gone something like this: *Dear Mrs. X., I appreciate your concern, as gratuitous as it might be, but I assure you that nothing in my household—no bill, no RSVP card, and most definitely no school project—has or ever will be sent in three weeks in advance. Now chill out, write a lesson plan, and rest easy knowing Jack will deliver the most stellar history of Rome presentation ever penned. Or at least a mediocre trifold display.*

What happened to the days of asking your kids if they're homework was done? "Yes? Great, g'night!" The most my parents had to do was sign report cards and a permission slip or two, and maybe help with the story problem that had me in tears. Millennial parents are totally screwed. School is more bureaucratic than the IRS, with signature requirements, checks needed for book fairs, candy-o-gram forms, and a hundred different little projects. In one month I've had to create a footlong boat, decorate a turkey in ways that symbolize our family culture (who makes this stuff up?!), and write two hand-written notes as my children's "pen pal," thanks to another stellar program initiated by an overmedicated PTO president. Someone please introduce this woman to a cause. Dolphins, the carbon footprint—anything but more parent-centric activity. And who on the green earth do they think makes these projects for first graders? Kenai can hardly wipe his butt let alone construct a watercraft with raw materials.

And it only gets worse as they grow older. For anyone challenged by math, you're done. You had a good run, but it's time to hire a tutor. I've lost weeks of my life trying to figure out seventh-grade algebra problems (okay fifth-grade), literally giving up on a few and writing the teacher a note of apology: *Dear Mr. Thompson, please excuse Jack's missing problems. The right side of my brain is severely underdeveloped, and I'd stand a better chance at achieving world peace than assisting with problem number 14.*

Of course rather than write letters of anguish, you can always air your concerns in person during the ever-dreaded parent-teacher conferences. Oh, bittersweet pleasure of the PTC. This biannual event begins by you leaving work in the middle of the day for some awkward one-on-one time with your kids' teachers. I see the need when they're older. You want to make sure they're progressing, adjusting, learning at a good rate. But the kindergarten through third-grade conferences are just too much.

For me, these conferences consist of twenty minutes of me trying to appear very serious, as the teacher talks with the utmost intensity about my kid's ABC recognition. God bless these people. You'd think our five-year-olds were exploring life on other planets. "Kenai is *really* showing initiative with learning his sight words, and really progressing with his numbers." *We're talking about the same kid who still pees himself once a week, right?* It's probably because I don't have the "teacher gene," but I find it so hard to take seriously. Of course I'd rather clean sewers than teach first grade.

And let's not forget the most overlooked, underappreciated school task that is the making of the lunches, lovingly prepared by executive chef mama at 9:30 p.m. with one eye open each night. No amount of blasting Kim Walker-Smith's Pandora station makes this assembly line of joy a rewarding experience. Although there are exceptions. I have a friend with six kids who makes a regular practice of posting a photo of her homemade, aesthetically pleasing lunch lineup on Instagram. And Facebook. Each day a different ensemble, but always with a fresh side of arugula-mandarin salad. I'm happy her children are experiencing culinary magic at lunchtime, but stuff like this drives me into deep dejection, comparing this to the squished Ziploc bags of pepperoni wraps and PB&J my kids pull out every day. I'm always tempted to upload a photo of three Lunchables with the caption: "Lunches are done—time for a bath!" I know I'd get more likes.

Managing school activities and requirements can be exhausting, but I've found some helpful tips and tactics to help maintain sanity, especially with school-aged kids:

- Always. And I mean always, plan outfits (socks are the key!), pack lunches, hunt down school library books, sign homework, complete permission slips, and find any necessary money the night before. There is nothing worse than Dumpster diving in the couch for hot lunch quarters at 7:30 a.m. "Who took the singles out of my purse?!" or cringing as your first grader boards the bus with flagrantly mismatched socks. "Navy and turquoise are both in the blue family, honey—now run!"

- Resist the overwhelming temptation to ignore school and teacher newsletters. If you can fight your way past the clip art, emojis, and superfluous details about which life cycles, seasons, sight words, and number charts your child is learning at that exact moment in time, you'll find some informational treasures. I deleted all e-newsletters until standing at the bus stop not once, but twice, in total ignorance that it was a professional development day. *Where is that bus?*

- Turn homework time into quality time, especially if you have more than one child, where it can be difficult giving them undivided attention. Even when they don't necessarily need help, I think kids like knowing you're there and their work matters to us. Sometimes it can be the only twenty minutes of alone time you really spend together.

- Try to bang out the homework before dinner, or right after dinner, if the kids have after-school activities. There are few weeknight surprises as frustrating as your child announcing he has an extra homework page, reading assignment, or heaven help us, some kind of project he "forgot" about at 8:00 p.m. Any mother cutting up library-loaned magazines (Jesus forgives) in search of warm climate amphibians need only learn this lesson once.

CHAPTER 17

"Mom, We Want a Puppy," and Other Words That Will Ruin Your Life

There is a graveyard in the sky full of furry martyrs falling prey to the same fate: being embraced as pets in the Kastner household. Sad to say, more of God's creatures have probably died under our roof than all our local interstates combined.

Like many domestic delusions of grandeur, adding a pet to the mix when you're already overwhelmed with family life is like throwing a living, breathing wrench into your wheel of insanity, and unfortunately, they suffer and die. Needless to say, we're not getting this year's PETA award.

Getting a dog, or other high-maintenance pets like rabbits that poop constantly, is just a symptom of the same disease that led many of us to believe buying a minivan was some kind of vehicular passageway into parenthood. But then after the enchantment of having DVD hookups fades, you realize you're driving *a van*, and you're like, *This is ridiculous. I'm not a Cox cableman.* Other lofty ideals and ideas like buying a $200 juicer to make organic baby food, jumping on the cloth-diaper train, and signing your soul off to Cub Scout masterhood all fall into this category of delusional decision making.

It's not that I haven't witnessed happy family pet owners, in the same way that some parents drive their Odysseys with nothing but pride. "The smoothness of those sliding rear doors!" Like a steel-winged eagle. For our family, however, I think our pet problems stemmed from the fact that all our kids were "accidents" and we were overwhelmed by each blessed addition. So when the boys, at ten, three, and two, begged to fill the vacuous hole in our home that could only be filled with a puppy, we caved, and we lived with a deep regret named "Buddy."

Ah, Buddy. Just as the minivan did not become many parents' chariot of dreams, and the tablet did not become the children's "learning tool," Buddy in no way filled a dog-shaped heart etched in our souls. Buddy was the most out-of-control, high-maintenance, exasperating example of irrational decision making on four legs.

Fresh out of the mobile rescue shelter at our local Petco, Buddy was half Australian shepherd and half Satan. But darn was he cute. All it took was his doofy grin and four rescue-working zealots assuring us we'd be sowing good karma into the fabric of the universe for fulfilling Buddy's destiny, and the deal was done. *I thought we were just looking for a cheap alternative, but I'll take it!*

I still cannot believe the bureaucracy and ridiculousness involved with millennial pet adoptions. In my day, people placed ads in the paper selling puppies or kittens on a first-come, first-serve basis to anyone without the appearance of a serial killer. When in the world did it become necessary to provide veterinary references before even "adopting" (on behalf of human orphans everywhere, please find another term) these creatures? Unbelievable.

We had to give our socioeconomic stats and square-foot dimensions, and offer a written promise to love and treasure our new family member for all eternity, or in the event of an unbeknownst dog allergy, find a home with a synonymous level of pet psychosis. We're talking about this dog here, who sat in his own poop, right? But as with so many of life's red-taped adventures, we smile, we oblige, and we squelch the urge to relay that we'll try our derndest to feed them once a day, always flush in the probable case they drink out of the toilet, and never, ever physically abuse them after they devour our new Nikes.

Who rescued who? I did, Buddy, and you're lucky you're alive after chewing through my cell charger.

Just as the stage of infancy begins, it always starts out fine. Our furball of wonder, freshly spared from riding back to rescue headquarters in a Subaru covered in "Coexist" stickers and rainbow flags, slept a lot, made those little puppy sounds, and absolutely brought joy into the family. For about five months. Until we sold him on Craigslist. I dunno. Maybe it was my estrogen imbalances, or the fact that Buddy could not control his urge to relieve his pea-sized bladder on every square inch of carpet. I was still changing two toddlers' diapers, and Buddy's fate quite simply came down to the fact that there was just one too many creatures taking craps on my watch.

That, when coupled with the incessant barking, digging more holes in the yard than a minefield, and the worst of it all, begging for my attention during the boys' naptime, was just too much. Poor Buddy. He was just a puppy in need of some shrapnel of affection.

How was he to know that seeking even one ounce of energy from a mother of three boys was like trying to suck sap out of a dead maple. To me, this was just one more being I felt guilty for not paying enough attention to. Of course I want to go for a run with you, Buddy, but I have to answer fifty emails before naptime's over. Let me introduce you to the garage …

Despite the irritating guilt trips, pee stains, and shoe pillaging, I was still in the game until sweet Buddy committed the reprehensible act of treason that has sent so many pets back on the market: he woke the kids from naptime—repeatedly. It's like putting up with a bad relationship until you catch your man cheating. Aw, heck no. Pack those bags.

Yes, getting a pet when you're already in over your head is bad for everyone, and no parent should feel guilty for either saying "Wait 'til you can walk them, or care for them, yourself" or sticking to fish and turtles. Since childhood I have marked the graves of two geckos, three hermit crabs, a cat that suffocated on fabric softener (we saw the bite marks), a rabbit whom my stepdad clocked over the head with a shovel because he thought he was diseased, a Lhasa apso that became deranged after getting hit with a baseball at a family picnic, and two cats that lost to games of chicken with the neighbor's Volvo.

So it was with determination and a renewed sense of hope that we "rescued" two kittens this year, in round fifteen of pet survivor, and things were looking up. Until Snowball began consistently confusing every inch of the house for a litter box. For anyone never experiencing the unique potency and stench of cat pee, I apologize that my words will fail to convey the stink. When mixed with the distinct odor of his incessant spraying, despite the fact that he was neutered, it was intolerable. We gave him a month to get his act together, before taking to Craigslist yet again with "free kitty to loving home."

I felt bad for yet another pet fail, but Snowball's legacy continued. Although both cats were "fixed," according to the shelter, my remaining cat birthed kittens looking exactly like Snowball two months later. My kids called this immaculate kitty conception "Snowball's revenge," which was hilarious until each kitten slowly died, one after another, turning our house into a haven of death filled with crying kids and kitty funerals, complete with Bible readings. Terrible.

God made plants and animals and called them good, and I believe pets are his way of making sure no one's alone in this world. However, before purchasing a living creature out of guilt or naive enthusiasm, consider goldfish. Truly. Phenomenal creatures.

THIS IS WHAT HAPPENS WHEN YOU'VE GIVEN UP PERFECTION

CHAPTER 18

The Case of the Strong-Willed Child: I Think My Quiver Is Full

When I was a single, newly Christian mom, a church matriarch took me under her wing and insisted I attend her group studying the "Growing Kids God's Way" curriculum. I found myself surrounded by similarly wide-eyed parents equipped with our workbooks and determination to raise obedient children who would bloom in our parenting garden of glory. I can still hear the haunting echoes of her five kids locked in their basement as we studied discipline and child-rearing techniques during our ninety-minute sessions. I remember thinking all the fear mongering about how to handle disobedience and willfulness was a bit much. Have a little faith, people.

But I knew no better. My first was a sweet, docile child who would pull a U-turn at the mere mention of a spanking. I grew him God's way, and clearly I was a master gardener. So I'd be that mom at the library pitying the obviously inept mother lassoing her wild boar of an offspring to get him out the door. I'd watch the parents argue and debate with their kids through stores, just wishing I could help them put their feet down and show some God-given authority.

Then I had my second child, and all my inward mocking came back to haunt me. Eli took his first breath, looked around, and thought, *I shall rule these minions.* My first stayed in his crib 'til age three. Eli at eighteen months was jumping out and storming his door barricade like a French revolutionist. My first would ask, "How many veggies should I eat today, Mommy?" Eli still refuses to wear underwear, based on the self-realized truth that it's a needless garment. He is seven.

Anyone questioning at this point whether they might have a strong-willed child, let me assure you, you do not. You'd know if you did. I had no idea a human being weighing fewer than thirty pounds could exert such self-assertion and determination. It's not even that he's badly behaved. He's just … independent (my coping mechanism is denial). Nothing, not a thing on this planet, is simple with a willful one. I would ask Eli to sit next to me and enjoy a castle-sized ice cream with Batman himself, and he'd furrow his brow and insist on a different flavor. I try to look at it in a positive light, hoping God will mold this obstinacy into great leadership skills someday.

This is all very embarrassing behavior, especially in Christian circles, where having control over your children seems to be an outward statement of Christ's reign in your home. There's no better way to gain looks of pity from your parenting peers than your kid screaming "I'm not going upstairs, EVER!" in the middle of Tuesday night's life group. They say they're praying for you, but we know what they're thinking: *Maybe if she put as much work into parenting as she does at the gym every day …*

What your Bible study mates do not understand is if Mommy doesn't work out her angst on the glute machine daily, she might go shopping for produce one day and never come back.

Even more trying than the fatigue brought on by such stubbornness is the humiliation. Is there anything more humbling than bartering with your child in public to avoid the ever-dreaded tantrum? I never thought I'd see the day. Example number 27 on my list of things I never thought I'd stoop to as a parent. I could win a Heisman for the number of times I've carried Eli out in a football hold, kicking away. (Helpful hint: feet first is more effective, to avoid blind kicks to strangers or siblings.) I have fallen facedown in a crowd with less humiliation than I feel when my child loses it in public. Lack of grace is understandable. Lack of discipline just screams, *"I am ruled by someone who soils their own pants!"*

I remember a particularly horrible experience at Blockbuster, baby number three in one hand, dragging Eli out with the other. Trying to ignore the judgmental stares from childless onlookers mentally placing bets on who would win this treacherous battle of wills. Ah, but the looks of shock only fueled Eli's fire. Now he had an audience. Let's throw some candy on the floor, lie facedown in classic spread-eagle position, and get this tantrum started. Always a crowd pleaser.

That outburst took a close second to one of our magical visits to our local library, where Eli threw a metal-based train (Percy, I believe) across the room in protest of our departure, hitting me directly in the forehead. My husband took one look at the dime-sized welt on my forehead and directly ordered takeout.

It's during such dark nights of the soul when you sink to the ultimate parental low: bribery. Never, ever had I sunk to such desperation with my first. I ask you, what kind of person promises toys in exchange for sitting on the potty? A potty surrounded by candy for the taking with just one squirt of pee? Surely any parent with mid-grade intelligence could think of better ways to persuade someone who regularly eats dirt. At three and a half (three and a half!!!) Eli's stubborn bahunkas had not once skimmed the surface of that pot. By the way, when in potty-training doubt, know this: your kid's too old for diapers when he's able to utter such a sentence, spoken by Eli during a diaper change: *"Today let's do something special and celebrate."* Three-syllable words should never transpire mid-wipe.

And this Truman-esque stubbornness has only worsened with age. Getting Eli into kindergarten after declaring he would not, in fact, be joining the educated masses was a miracle. His response to all of our persuasions was a calm "Sorry, guys. I'm not doin' it." No emotional discourse. No ensuing debate. He decided after much research that he would be better off homeschooled like his cousins, and there would be no need for a democratic vote. After much prayer and bribery he did join the laypeople come September, and I still feel ripples of relief to this day.

To those who say miracles are a thing of the past, I say rubbish. If I witnessed the Red Sea parting tomorrow, it would be with less incredulity than watching Eli wave good-bye that blessed morn. Praise 'em.

Difficult children can stretch you in ways you never thought possible, but God will provide the guidance on how to steer them, if you pray for patience and endless mental strength. The key is sticking to your guns when they become defiant, without speaking or acting out of anger. Discipline is like dieting. No one likes to do it, but the end result is always worth the work. One woman's lil' black dress is another woman's toddler sitting still in line. And like dieting, successful discipline really depends on your own self-discipline. It sure is easier to resist the butter pecan squares looming in the kitchen than dragging your kid out of Friendly's for crawling under the table.

"But we didn't even get our sundaes, Mom!!"

"Tell it to the E. coli, buddy. Check, please."

It can be so hard, and immensely aggravating, having to continually correct or punish, instead of "keeping the peace" by tolerating disobedience because you're too tired or busy to deal. But I've noticed through the years, when my kids get out of control, or stop listening, it's always because I've been lazy about enforcing consequences. I don't want to deal with the howling and grumbling that ensues after taking away the tablet, and I've even pretended not to notice disobedience at times, when my bath is half-filled and the last thing I want to do is bust a kid for carteling crackers into his bed after hours. *Look away thine eyes. Your spa awaits.*

But sticking to your guns, and really never, ever choosing momentary peace and convenience over tolerating disobedience, pays off big time in the long run. I've bitterly left many a party or playdate after dropping the hammer and leaving to endure mind-numbing vehicular tantrums. But I've found if you discipline consistently, starting at the ripe age of one, the need for it gets less and less, and you'll benefit from well-adjusted, happy kids. If we think "big picture" when it comes to discipline, remembering every time we don't budge—even when it's as simple as not allowing dessert when they don't eat the veggies—it pays off tenfold. They *will* eventually learn to obey, whine less, not talk back, listen better, etc., and life will be ohhhhh so much sweeter.

Here are some tips for creating un-brats:

Nip It in the Bud

I mean seriously, drop the hammer the second you see behavior in your kids that needs correcting. If you notice your kindergartener suddenly talk with an attitude, don't let it go on for months before sitting down and explaining what needs to change. If your one-year-old starts yelling "Mine!" and grabbing every tangible commodity in his wake, correct him every time, before he's "that baby" in the church nursery hoarding the Cheerios. This goes for all ages. Just because you've nipped talking back in the bud doesn't mean you're not gonna be dealing with "white lying" in a few months. It can be exhausting, but the quicker you put the kibosh on eye rolling, the better. I think the remnants of my jaw might still be on the Astroturf after recently witnessing Kenai's flag football teammate yelling "Shut up, Mom!" to his sideline-shouting mother during practice.

Fight the Anger

Ever come across a really nasty, angry kid, and all mysteries are solved upon meeting their hotheaded parents? *Ah. There you go.* Parents who handle their kids in anger usually produce angry kids. Being a disciplinarian doesn't mean you're a loveless drill sergeant losing your cool every time you count past three before your kids comes a runnin'. I've known parents who would brag about how many times they spanked their kids in a day like they were target shooting at the range. *Impressive. I'm sure they'll have zero repressed emotions 'til they're fifty.*

We've all lost our tempers and near consciousness after realizing our three-year-old knifed through brand-new Sephora bronzer with a Play-Doh tool, but the goal should be as little shouting and anger as possible. When you feel the blood a boilin', it's best to send them to their room, even if it means you need two minutes to cool off. If you're in public, and feel you're one tantrum away from showing the town library your Italian side, I've always packed it up and dealt with the kids when we're home. No matter what. You're not gonna scream and yell, but there will absolutely be consequences. If you struggle with your temper, like I did, pray constantly for the Holy Spirit to fill you with self-control, patience, and enough grace to get through the Target line without beating your kids with the Skittles package they're demanding. And in the rare moment of parental weakness you act out in anger, I think it's a good idea to apologize to the kids for yelling, showing them no one's perfect and we all need God's help. So much. So much help.

CHAPTER 19

Breaking the Law with the Kids in the Backseat, and Other Moral Dilemmas

I am a chronic offender of my state's motor vehicle department. At least since 2005, when they deemed it illegal to use handheld cell phones while driving. Not only a pathetic way to increase state revenue, but in my opinion, a direct hit to the mommy sector of the community. I rebel against this law on sheer principle, and maybe a tad for convenience. Because mothers with kids are so busy they can barely get a minute of privacy on the toilet let alone make insurance adjustments over the phone for fifteen minutes.

And kids have the keen ability to sense the second you get on the phone. Suddenly they need juice, they're fighting over a toy neither of them wanted a minute ago, or they absolutely need me to pretend I'm the mommy dog. I've actually conversed with a friend in desperate need of advice while doubling as mommy dog. "You deserve—*ruff ruff*—better, and they need to compensate you—*bow wow*—based on your performance. *Ruff.*" So those ten-to-fifteen-minute car rides can be the only time (besides precious naptime when we have to work, shower, exercise, etc.) to talk on the phone. Sorry, Officer, but have you smelled me lately?

This said, there comes a time when your children get older and become, well, aware of your less-than-upstanding habits and call you out on them. It's shocking at first. Jack at five years old: "Mom, don't the police arrest people for talking on their phones in the car?" "Mom, if the speed limit is thirty-five, why are you going fifty?" "Why did you tell the person on the phone Mrs. Kastner is not home now?"

Hmmmmm. This new phase of life posed quite an irritating crisis of conscience for me. On the one hand, I could explain that even the police don't expect us to drive thirty-five on East Street and the no-trespassing signs are only for people who don't live in the neighborhood, but those aren't quite true. I tend to be flawed in the white-lie department when it comes to my kids, so I struggle on this one. I try to curb my unlawfulness by picturing Jack at sixteen going a hundred miles per hour on the freeway: "It's cool, guys. My mom speeds all the time!" But my inner road rage prohibits me from driving forty miles per hour. Ever.

It gets even better when they live to tell about it. Proving God has a sense of humor, Jack has the memory of an elephant. "Mom, remember that time you got pulled over two times in one week in the red car?" And soon, you actually have to practice what you preach. Can't get rid of that temper problem? Have a kid. After an angry phone dispute with customer service, I was greeted by a very somber seven-year-old: "Mom, Jesus says getting angry is the same as killing someone." *Ouch.*

This heightened sense of justice can be a buzzkill if you have a "worrier" child. Explaining to Eli for the fifth time that the police will not arrest us for sneaking Pop Secret into the movies isn't even worth saving the six bucks. Previous practices such as cramming four (okay, five) kids in the backseat to avoid carpooling are a bit tougher when you have to explain your degeneracy to your fretful five-year-old. "Honey, we're only going to Auntie Jill's, and you all have your seat belts on." "But, Mom, the police will arrest us!!!"

The list goes on of depressing ways kids keep us accountable and also make us realize how potentially white trash we've become. Oh, the temptation to buy the season passes half-off for your "under three" kid. "But, Mom, Kenai turned three in the summer!" RIGHT. It was with GREAT resistance that we bought two photo ID ski passes for children who could pass for twins. *Jesus, give me strength.*

Of all the soul-refinement kids bring us, I've found the death of the white lie to be perhaps the most painful. I wasn't even aware I was guilty of this habit until my husband began catching me out: "Mama—*sniff, sniff*—are you gonna be home before we're asleep?" "Yeeeeees, honey." Is this true? Heck no. Will it prevent a meltdown and potential destruction of your tapas night with the girls? Absolutely. But my husband catches me every time and insists on total forthrightness. Ugh.

The inconvenient truth is, if we're expecting our kids to act respectfully and obediently, we have to be the example. How many times have I exited an argument with my husband, or spent way too long complaining about something to a friend on the phone, and then caught my kids speaking in disrespectful tones that same day? The brutal early years of marriage with all their romance, charm, and passionate fighting taught me that, despite my emotions, I couldn't stoop to behavior I'm punishing my kids for. We can't compartmentalize our lives, thinking we can act out of the character of God, and expect our kids to listen to us blindly, without picking up our own bad habits. If we tell them to be kind to the annoying kid on the bus, but then they hear us ripping the oil company a new one over the phone for overcharging us, we've wasted our time.

Same goes for all our annoying habits. One particularly dark day of self-realization led me to notice everything I was criticizing Jack for; his procrastination, general slop, and saying "Yeah, I'll do that" with no follow-through were literally my own faults staring back at me. I've stood knee-deep in my own bedroom clutter, nagging this boy to clean his room, and literally stopped midsentence. "Okay, ya know what? Never mind." Every time I find myself doing anything out of the will of God, I immediately think, would I want my kid doing, watching, wearing, saying, or doing this when he's my age? I hope not. But they're watching and learning by us now, so unfortunately for the HBO series that we've been loving and ignoring conviction about, it's time to live like we want our kids to, starting now. I'm lookin' at you, *Game of Thrones*.

CHAPTER 20

The Proverbs 31 Wife: Now That's a Bit Much

I think the pressures of being the perfect wife and mother are so much more acute in Christian circles. First of all, we grew up with Proverbs 31 as our goal: a type-A woman who wakes "earlier than the night," working 'round the clock, doing good to her man, and earning the praises of her children daily. Sigh.

For Christmas one year, my sister gave me a wall decor saying: "Boring Women Have Immaculate Houses." I of course embraced it as gospel and hung it on my wall, but then it bothered me—the fact that people were buying signage based on my failed domesticity.

Fact is, I'm messy. I've always been scattered and unorganized (a trait omitted from my LinkedIn profile, of course), and it only got worse when I had kids. The responsibility for the order of an entire family is overwhelming. Suddenly it's not just *your* disgusting car that no one ever sets foot in. Other people's children have to climb into my junk-filled caboose when carpooling, and it's humiliating. Motherhood seemed to instantly make my bad habits more socially offensive.

But staying neat and running an orderly home seems impossible to some of us "un-moms." The sanitation of my toilets and floors don't warrant DCF involvement, but when it comes to anything under the domestic sun—cooking, laundering, keeping toys organized—I am a total failure, especially compared to certain friends (refer to full-makeup mom in chapter 4) whose homes are gleaming beacons of neatness at all times. And it doesn't help that most of these Christian buddies homeschool their children, managing to teach foreign languages and cultural enrichment before lunchtime. I'm pretty sure they solve world peace in the afternoons while decluttering the basements.

One of these domestic divas actually had an intervention for me after house-sitting for my mom one summer. Sure, there were seemingly permanent Play-Doh shreds encrusted on a couch or two, and the Jacuzzi was clogged with toy carnage, but was this cause for panic? My friend's response: "Girl, your mama is not going to let you ever visit again if I don't help. Look at those baseboards!" Okay, she had a point. *But who looks at other people's baseboards anyways? Psycho.*

Nonetheless, it was with great shame as I watched Queen Clean achieve a whiteness in my shower I had not thought possible, *while* simultaneously cooking homemade Italian wedding soup—to deliver to a homebound church member, of course. She was like a gloved ninja, scrubbing in all directions and finding attachments on my vacuum I never knew existed.

She and other clear overachievers have given advice when I complain of my disorder, but nothing helps.

"Get a whiteboard and mark down your kids' chores, so everything gets done."

"Get a planner, and make a cleaning chart for yourself."

"Don't go to bed until your house is clean enough for visitors the next morning."

Well, I bought a table-sized whiteboard, lost the markers in two days, used the planner for a week before turning it into a therapy journal, and achieved REM amid clutter every night. *Morning visitors? Is this 1942?*

I know cleanliness is next to godliness, but God and I have it all worked out. I gave up trashy TV, and he tolerates the soap scum. We're good.

But it's hard not to feel like an underdeveloped being around such friends, feeling like I'm still learning how to be a real woman. A Proverbs 31 gal. My friend wore an apron at home 24/7, packed with a "sad spoon" for paddling (six kids, people; no judgment) and a cordless phone to answer her husband's business calls. Her kids were trained for household duties early on, sorting laundry, unloading the dishwasher, and even tilling soil. I swear she breeds for efficiency.

Her house looks like a child labor camp compared to my children's shameless lack of responsibility. I don't know where I went wrong. Heck, my sister has given me laminated checklists (yes, she owns a laminating machine) and many, many parenting books. But somehow I'm the one at the end of the night tossing toys into bins and staring at their messy rooms in disgust. Jack does some chores, but it's rather painful to witness. Snails could mow the lawn faster, and he basically abuses our local water sources, taking forty-five minutes to wash the dishes each night. I dunno.

We want to give our kids a sense of structure and order, but mostly we sail through the days on survival mode, schlepping them from dinner to homework to baths, with a wake of socks, crayons, and sippy cups behind us. Every night it's an army crawl into bed, vowing we'll do things better, and praying for more patience and efficiency the next day.

But I think the older we get, the more comfortable we become with our parenting styles and the less we compare ourselves to others. I have gifts that just don't shine so much through tangible domesticity. You know your limitations, rely on God for help, and celebrate what makes you great. Yes, I recently baked peanut-butter-cup brownies without removing the wrappers, but I've also woken my kids up out of a cold sleep to stargaze on the deck and revel at God's wonder. They go to school at least once a week with different socks, and they still think potatoes come in a box. But not a week goes by that we don't have a sweat-'til-ya-drop worship party that always commences with the youngest getting buck naked and screaming, "It's booty-shaking time!"

Truth is, half the time our kids don't notice our parental short-falls. I don't think they'll look back and remember the perfectly folded shirts, or how tender the flank steak was. I'm hoping they'll look back and remember our barefooted "happy parades" in the backyard and the wild, messy love we tried our best to give. There'll be plenty of good pot roast in heaven, I s'pose.

CHAPTER 21

The Multitasking Puppeteer: Because Daddy Could Never Pull This Off

Women are amazing. We know this. I tend to shy away from gender comparisons, but we simply have some gifts that men don't, and vice versa. We're great listeners and nurturers, and we have incredible inner strength. But once you become a mother, it's like an entire slew of talents are birthed—and you need them all, for survival. To me, the most vital of these gifts is the art, the necessity, of multitasking.

I first became aware of this maternal talent when finishing college as a single mom. I was determined to breastfeed, but the three-hour classes were merciless on my bursting boobs. This led to the quickly acquired art of pumping with my state-of-the-art Medela while driving home on the interstate. I might have frightened and perhaps entertained a trucker or two, and even gotten a ticket through this process, but damn was I good. I could get a solid eight ounces before my exit.

Flash forward a couple of years, and my multitasking feats only improved. Any mother knows the need to keep baby awake during late-morning car rides if there's any chance of a nap. My answer to this anti-sleep challenge is to present Emmy-quality puppet shows, while driving. Again, slightly shameful, but my chances at being the DMV's poster child were over by age seventeen. All I need is a stuffed animal, or even a sock, and I'm Shari Lewis on wheels. My husband can't mix batter while humming a tune, but I can make Bob the Tomato tango on a headrest while navigating homeward. Sorry, honey, but it's true.

The list goes on, doesn't it? The number of times we've transformed into sword-fighting Power Rangers with one kid while answering an eternal litany of questions being asked by another, or putting on full makeup while pretending to be Bob the Builder. I've seen mom friends close business deals while climbing a Playscape. Don't believe me, fellas? I'll take it a step further. I remember trying to keep up with my husband's "romantic" (okay, dirty) texts while pretending to be a T-Rex. I remember thinking, *If only he knew I was squatting over invisible dino eggs while promising to "have fun" later with that red lacy thing*. Incredible. Really, can anyone justly describe the lunacy that goes on behind the doors of casa de mama?

But all this is child's play in the multitasking department when compared to the unbelievable juggling efforts it takes working from home. In a rare moment of insanity, I decided I could write a story for an online newspaper every day. One baby was nine months; the other was two. I don't know what I was thinking. I've made crazy life choices earlier in life, but they were usually preceded by some homegrown herb or straight tequila. This was a sober decision made with Tony Robbins–esque confidence. *I'm a hustler. A woman with her pen, to be stopped by nothing.*

In a matter of days, my life turned into what I can only describe as the ninth circle of Dante's hell. At any given point in the day my phone would ring and I would interview local and state politicians

and leaders—people who may have forgotten the endearing quality of screaming children in the background. I remember nervously
speaking with a senator as my youngest drew blood while gnawing on
my bare leg with all his might. And whenever it seems safe to make
a business call—*Blue's Clues* was working her magic with a lineup of
perishables—they'll immediately run over, crying or attacking each
other. Sometimes it breaks the ice with people, "Oh, I hear you have
little ones over there!" but others are less enthused. I always remind
myself how great it is to have them home all day, leg wounds and all.
But their daddy could never do this. Just sayin'.

Multitasking is a gift, but I think sometimes we can teeter between
being industrious and being just plain chaotic. Somewhere between
watching my car get towed after forgetting to renew my registration,
and missing parent-teacher conferences, again, God started showing
me that maybe my hurried, fly-by-the-seat "way" wasn't quite his
will. I've been really asking God to help me be more purposeful with
my time, not taking on that one extra task or insisting on squeezing
an activity in before the next. As mothers, it's almost impossible to
handle this modern lifestyle without being a little out of control.
We're expected to be great spouses, mothers, employees, cooks (so
I've heard), school and ministry volunteers, etc., and still remember
to refill the home-heating oil and visit Gramma on her birthday.
But I've realized more and more my chaotic way of life may not be
great for my kids, or my mental health. I think of all the mornings
I've parachuted the boys from the car on the way to school, rushed
them through activities because I didn't plan ahead well enough,
and really created a general state of disarray and urgency that doesn't
exactly instill security and peace, or offer a good example of how to

be an adult. Rushing may be an unavoidable consequence of living in westernized culture, but when your children come to view the police as the enemy because they've given Mommy so many tickets, it may be time to readjust.

I'm admittedly just at the beginning stages, but for all the multitasking ball jugglers out there, there is a way. First, ask God to give you the desire to slow down, on a daily basis. Pray whether everything you've committed to, or are involved in, is in his will, and make the necessary adjustments. Do you really need to go to the gym six days a week? Do you need to cut down on phone chats with friends? How 'bout Facebook? Whenever you feel yourself about to take on too much—if it's thinking you can cook dinner before picking up the kids from soccer at 5:20—fight the urge and save a burnt pot. When the kids get off the bus in ten minutes, resist taking a work call you know will last forever. Ask God to help you figure out how to establish more order in your house, whether it's making the kids more responsible for chores or literally scheduling blocks of time for things like getting things ready the night before to avoid the before-work or -school insanity that ensues when forgetting to make lunches, iron, or find school or store money or those blasted school library books that should, in all seriousness, come with tracking devices.

The toughest challenge can be making extra time and plan ahead. I get it. I have mental street duals with the clock. *Oh yeah, 11:00 a.m. volunteer orientation meeting? Think you can stop me from grocery shopping before then? Bring it.* I've forced myself to resist decade-long patterns of leaving everything to the last minute, like organizing pre-sentation materials the night before to avoiding tearing closets apart in search of Sharpies and name tags … *"Who does this?!"* Time management is a beast, but God really does want more peace for us in this life. It's a journey, but we can get there. Here's to lunches made the night before, garbage nights never missed, and never, ever speeding and being chased for miles by the police, after blasting Hillsong so loud you didn't notice. Hope for all, I tell you.

THIS IS WHAT THEY'LL EXPOSE YOU TO

CHAPTER 22

The Playdate Heard 'Round the World

Another aspect of parenthood that blindsides you is an inevitable unpleasantry known as other people's kids. We've all been on that tense playdate with a friend whose kids make the Taliban seem civilized. You try to be understanding of your girlfriend's laissez-faire parenting ... until her kid throws sand in your kid's face for the third time. Oh yeah. He's goin' down. I'm not making a case for the almighty spank—I'm just asking for some stern reprieves or apologies. I've sat in forty-five-minute minivan rides listening in anguish to friends' children mouthing off and hurling insults, aka being "fresh," in their mommy's words. Eggs are fresh. These kids are demons.

And slowly, the realization hits you: a good friend doth not make a good mother. Other people's parenting styles have shocked the heck outta me. Like fashion, some styles are on trend, some should remain in the eighties. I've narrowed down my experiences to four categories so far:

The Yes Man
Once at a park I overheard a stay-at-home dad describe his parenting style. In a nutshell, he doesn't like to use the word no. Instead,

he'll suggest alternatives to what his child is asking for. And I know someone who actually adheres to this. Just once I want to watch what happens when their kid's running full tilt toward the road: "N— I mean, why don't you veer to the right, sweetheart, or you'll be a heaping pile of roadkill!" Maybe I'm being narrow minded. The problem is that these continually affirmed children grow up and might be a bit underprepared for the amount of noes they'll hear in life. If they get married, it'll be an everyday occurrence. Hope those alternatives keep ya warm at night, kid, because it's gonna be a heck of a journey past five.

The Mommy in Denial

This is a frightening variety of mother who can literally carry on a thirty-minute conversation while her kids wreak havoc on the world. I don't know how they block it out, but it's borderline sociopathic. I've sat with a friend while her children literally beat the snot out of each other ten feet away, without her blinking an eye. Just kept on sipping the soy decaf latte and discussed a new book in Zen-like state of relaxation. You and other bystanders find this disturbing, of course, but who wants to be the buzzkiller? "Hey, uh, *oh*, that was a bite—are your boys okay?" *Siiiiiip.* Same thing when you talk with these friends over the phone, with their children wailing in the background like a mourning procession. "Oh my gosh, do you have to go?!" "Oh no, the baby's just crabby. Anyways ..."

The Faker

This, to me, is the worst of 'em all. The mom who wages false threats and phony ultimatums to their crazy brats ... and then lets them get away with everything, including kicking your own kids. "Honey, stop kicking or you're not getting ice cream later!" "If you don't apologize, we're not going to the pool!" One chocolate sundae, and two hours of doggy paddling later, and the only one apologizing is me, for leaving the playdate early to escape her hellions. What part of Don't Ruin Your Kids 101 these moms missed is beyond me, but it is painful to witness. Even worse is when the uncontrolled naughtiness becomes contagious. It takes one time seeing my kids mimic the snotty attitude from their playmates, and I'm out. I didn't escape the terrible twos to lose the battle now.

The "Maybe I Should Call DCF" Mom

We've all known, or at least witnessed, this type yelling at their kids like an NFL coach from the sidelines. But this is not the 'Niners' home turf; this is the town park, and they're scaring every other kid in a one-hundred-foot radius. "GET OVER HERE RIGHT NOW OR YOU'RE GONNA REGRET IT!!" We all regret it, lady. Please make it stop. Maybe it's because my parents never really "yelled" or used sarcasm with us that I find it so intolerable. There must be a better way than going Kanye West on your kids at the FroYo.

All of this discomfort doesn't come close to the amount of awkwardness that arises when your kids don't want to play with your friend's children, simply because they're so terrifying. This is when things get tricky. The underground ring of parental politics that goes on makes *House of Cards* seem like a peace treaty. Avoiding the unwanted playdate is possible, but difficult.

"Oooh, I don't think we're in the beach mood today," or "I'm low on funds; I think we'll skip the museum, but thanks!" usually gets the job done. But the plot thickens if you have mutual friends. Try explaining yourself after getting caught "playing" with another mommy friend when you evaded the other. Darn you, Instagram. You want to tell your offended friend that her kids invoke terror in the hearts of men and your kids would rather eat cabbage than share a mutually occupied sandbox, but you can't.

We've all been through it. You finally score a mom friend who shares your level of devotion to caffeine and rarely blows you off for irregular napping schedules, and then ... the revelation comes: her children are literal terrors. They talk back, hurl insults at everyone standing in the wake of their emotional instability, and display all the early signs of serial killerhood. Sigh. This is a drastic example, but unfortunately our kids' friends, and people whom you put in their lives, have a big influence on their behavior. When we notice them making friends and being influenced by kids with disobedient and even nasty tendencies, we have to step in. They'll eventually be developed enough not to be influenced and copy the ways of the world, but they're small, and it's up to us to limit their exposure to bad influencers, even if it means the cool mom's kids. It can be just as difficult and even as uncomfortable when the kids get older and your teen starts hanging out with the wrong friends. Even if it's just a rude friend with an attitude, it helps to limit the friendship, if possible. The first time Jack started hanging with a twelve-year-old friend we affectionately coined "Punk Boy," I almost dropped dead hearing him talk smack from the basement on Xbox.

"Hey, Jack, whatever happened to Alex? He was such a nice boy ..."

CHAPTER 23

Children's Parties: Where Saturdays Go to Die

Anyone remember what weekends were like pre-kid? Reading in bed 'til 10:00, cleaning, brunch, going for a hike, the list goes on … until you procreate. It's not that baby kills the Saturday. You can still salvage some shred of weekend freedom postpartum. Perfectly possible to squeeze in squats during naptime or take baby to the farmer's market. It's when they reach preschool age that you're done. Those just entering parental bliss might question, what is this weekend killer you speak of? What could be so gruesome and dire as to put an end to the questionably best day of the week? Two words: Children's. Parties.

Where to begin. Let's start with a blast to the past, where parents aged twenty-five to fifty most likely remember what children's birthday parties used to be. You, and maybe one or two of your closest friends, got invited to your cousin's parties out of obligation. Celebratory events usually took place in the backyard or basement, followed by a variety of pizza or starch product, homemade Pillsbury, and then presents. Kids were gone by the third hour, thrilled with their Ziploc-turned-goodie bag stuffed with Skittles, Hubba Bubba, and maybe even stickers.

Present-day children's parties make these past functions look like third-world picnics. I don't know why or when children's parties began transforming into events fit for royalty, but they have, and it's awful.

First of all, who originated the all-inclusive madness of inviting every classmate, boy and girl, to their kid's birthday party? This is the reality you'll face upon school enrollment. Your child will most likely step off the bus in ecstatic expectation, with twenty invites a year. Let's pause for a little math. Even if you accept a modest half, that's a party nearly once a month. If you have one kid. I have three. Not to mention twenty-two cousins within a ten-mile area and two sisters with a combined total of eight children who all celebrate their first day of life. So there it is: my life on Saturdays is reduced to making sure my kid doesn't whack himself with a piñata bat. And on the off weekend, I'm shopping for the next one. Birthday parties are now a line item in the family budget.

But the expense isn't the worst part. It's the Herculean effort these parties demand. The kids might still be running through sprinklers high on Betty Crocker in some part of Alabama, but in New England, such nonsense won't fly.

Every kid's party typically offers at least several of the following: an inflatable bouncy house, catering, $50 bakery cakes, designer goodie bags, on-site pony rides, and the arrival of a Disney character. It's absolutely ridiculous. This isn't Prince George's christening, people; it's a one-year-old's party, and he's napping through most of it.

And then there's the off-site party destinations. In the last two years I've Google-mapped my way across the state in search of trampoline parks, an indoor water park, a horse farm, and a climbing gym five towns away. Not so torturous, it might seem, until your first encounter with the third circle of hell otherwise known as Chuck E. Cheese's. Sigh. For anyone visiting this establishment, I need not write a word. For those yet to encounter this labyrinth of dread, picture a two-thousand-square-foot facility with two hundred screaming children shoving overpriced tokens into age-inappropriate games, leaving a trail of boogers and tears when they lose. It's a loud, sweaty rabbit hole no one should befall. Also of note: they serve beer at 10:00 a.m., which attracts the very highest caliber of clientele, I assure you. Everyone is panic struck; some are searching for their lost kids stuck in Playscape netting; others are questioning their very existence. *How did I get here? I was supposed to have made partner by now, not hoarding hand sanitizer in a strip-mall-based fun center …*

And whether it's an off- or on-site function, here's another nugget of goodness: no one leaves their kids at the party anymore. The good old days of sending off your party-bound children and scoring two hours of "me time" are gone. I learned this fun fact the hard way with my first, when all the parents dropped their kids off … and never left my house. All my attempts, "Okay, so I'm thinking it'll be over around threeish," were to no avail. Not a budge. Now you have to order triple the amount of food, clean twice as hard, and make awkward small talk with the heavy-handed snack-eating dad who sticks around. Hey, Jamison's dad. Go to Home Depot. No one wants to steal your kid. Trust. Parents, if an invite arrives via school backpack, this party's not for you.

This brings us to the always memorable experience of holding your own party. Time to cash in on a year's worth of Walmart toy shopping, and don't think for a second there's one pony on this half acre of heaven. My parties have gotten better over the years, keeping up with whatever Jones I can manage. But no matter what, it's always stressful, last minute, and when compared to my sister's parties, near pathetic. My sister's kids' parties go something like this: read about ladybug theme party in *Parents*, plan accordingly for one month, and re-create an actual event to the tee, with homemade ladybug wings for all who attend. Polka-dot perfection, down to the bug juice and critter cake.

In the ten years I've been navigating my way through large family events, mine look something like this: start thinking about the event a week before, actually shop for food and decorations one day before, barrel around the house like a rabid animal until people arrive, and then pray nothing blows up.

It's a formula that had done me well until Eli's third birthday. It all started out as normal. I forgot a crucial lasagna ingredient, forcing my husband outbound in a blizzard for ricotta and candles, and the in-laws arrived too early, just as I shoved the last armful of clutter in the closet. All I remember is holding the lit birthday cake and suddenly smelling smoke. I was able to ignore my guests' shrieks quick enough to realize the entire left side of my hair was aflame, prompting me to beat myself senseless with a dish towel until all was well. It took two days before my head stopped reeking of burnt ends, but I think overall, the party was a hit. My sister may have thrown the best ladybug party in New England, but mine had a live light display.

It's so easy to fall into the trap of "keeping up with the Joneses" when it comes to kids' events, technology, and material things, but it's really all about the experience and the memories you have with your kids. You can buy them every trinket out there and give them the best parties, outfits, toys, vacations—but they really just want us. The few times I've gone "all out"' for a party, and even Christmas, I found myself so distracted and preoccupied with making sure everything was perfect, I didn't have as many special moments as I did during the times with less hoopla. Some of the best celebrations I've had with my kids have been just our family, doing something together outside or going to a favorite restaurant. The Joneses will always be there … our kids won't.

CHAPTER 24

Carnivals, Cub Scouts, and Circle Time: Proof of Your Devotion

There is a group of people out there in uniform whom I suspect is a national cult. The vote's still out. Until you have a firsthand account of attending a Cub Scouts meeting, you really can't prepare yourself for what lies ahead, aside from a $25 neckerchief. My supposition that scouting consisted of an occasional goodwill act and camping trip was like most parental expectations: horribly erroneous. What I discovered is the Boy Scouts of America is really a multi-tiered, amalgamated bureaucracy that makes the federal government seem simple. Achievements, electives, progress toward rank beads, badges, arrow points, and homemade family totems await the unknowing scout parent. Three-hour weekly meetings, endless fund-raising activities (who sells popcorn anymore?!), and the painstaking amount of time it takes earning that next coveted badge.

But ten community service projects later and there I was, a full-fledged scouter, marching in the Apple Harvest parade with Troop Crazymarchin' to the beat of a type-A drum. Yes, the scouting life is to be taken with the utmost earnestness, according to our impassioned scout leader—a forty-year-old engineer who stood before us in full uniform, talking with intense gravity about proper flag-folding techniques. I made the mistake of joking about buying a "homemade" bead totem, and you'd think I'd committed treason before their very eyes. Tough crowd.

I think as parents we'd like to believe we can craft our own family life, including and excluding whatever activities, people, and influences we see fit. But we never expect some of the situations and experiences kids expose us to, such as the mile-thick *Scouting* handbook. Better we don't know. Better we aren't informed that we'll spend hours of our lives voluntarily standing in manure at carnivals and county fairs and paying $10 for merry-go-round rides operated by questionably intoxicated sixteen-year-olds.

Clearly our vision of parenthood was sprinkled with delusion and fantasy. Because from years one to ten, these will be some of the familiar scenes and events you'd never, ever consider pre-kid: paying a $15 cover charge for a county fair, waiting in borderline freezing conditions to voluntarily get lost in a corn maze, tractor riding with thirty strangers to pick a $20 pumpkin, standing in agony during two-hour town parades, spending your entire summer in the noxious local pool, sitting for three hours to claim your spot at the drive-in movies, counting down the minutes to story time at the public library, and giddily circling "kids" events in your town paper. "Touch-a-Truck moved to noon on Saturday, hun; don't forget!"

I guess it's better to remain ignorant of the fact that we will, without fail, be forced to siphon up the McDonald's Playscape and sit among the E. coli with our acrophobic toddler for a solid year of our lives. In moments like these, as you sit in plastic filth, knees up to your ears, you find yourself asking God some very real questions: Why am I here? How come I don't feel joy, Lord? Is this my delayed penance for the borderline backsliding in '05?

It's not that there isn't any joy and amazing memories found in all of these experiences. Watching Jack nearly faint with joy while hugging "Scoop" the dump truck is a visual I'll never forget. And although I'm still traumatized from the fifteen seconds we couldn't find Eli after exiting the Tilt-a-Whirl, I've admittedly had moments of pure, deep-fried fun at the town fair. In a way, I see the circumstances I'd formerly avoid but now embrace as more proof of the miraculous ways kids transform us. I recently witnessed a dad at the Magic Kingdom making the very most of a live, interactive dance show led by Buzz Lightyear himself. This man-picture of George from *Seinfeld* was doing the "watch me whip/nae nae" with his kids like his life depended on it. I mean, every step, hands in the air like he just don't care, kind of boogying, in front of hundreds of onlooking strangers with a smile wider than Texas. He paid $500 to get the fam through those rodent gates, sacrificed the yearly golfing trip for this nonsense, and dern it, he was getting his Disney on. Priceless.

I guess it's all about embracing the good, the bad, and the plastic, knowing you didn't parent by the sideline. The good memories and sacrifices are always worth it. I remind myself of this every Tuesday on my way to sacrifice the goat at Cub Scouts.

CHAPTER 25

Wanted: Mom Friend with a Tolerance for Filth

As much as un-moms have a hard time matriculating into certain die-hard mommy circles, there's a very real need for mom friends, and an unshakable bond that forms when you find one. One of the first things I did after recovering from the shock that my husband's Michael Phelpsian sperm had impregnated me with my third was to perform a mental scan of all friends who either had babies, were trying to conceive, or could be unknowingly knocked up after being as conceptually irresponsible as we were. *Katie's been a hot mess lately ... Maybe she's prego.*

Because being home alone with babies, with no one to meet you at the mall, park, pool, library, bounce gym, etc., is frankly terrifying. Sitting alone in a sandbox while your little one digs intently for an hour, watching all the other mom friends pull up together with community snacks and a week's worth of chatter to catch up on, is just so sad. This was my life with my first, and there was no way I was flying solo this next time around.

Thank God I managed to make a new mom friend (Arielle, you're my hero) who was not only pregnant, but carrying twins, thus

making her even more desperate than I was for daytime companion-
ship. I might not have seen her 'til she resurrected her mental and
physical fortitude six months after birth, but after that, I finally had
someone to call during that eternal 9-to-5 window—"I *have* to get
out of this house. Park in twenty minutes?!"—and someone who
understood the level of crazy I called home.

I've found the key to a good mom friend is finding one who
cares just as little for domestic perfection as you do, is spontaneous
enough to socialize on a moment's notice for emergency counseling
sess— I mean, playdates, and believes the entire purpose of getting
together has nothing to do with the children. I tell you, there are few
things so valuable in this world as a mom friend who doesn't judge,
let alone bat an eye when entering your house in the most debased
state of filth on a spur-of-the-moment playdate. You feel a tinge of
shame the first few times she catches you in your "real" state of living,
until you realize she's not only unfazed by the wreckage but lives in a
similar state of survival. You've found yourself a friend for life. Your
excuses go from "Yeah, come over but it's *really* disgusting right now"
to "Yes! Come over. We've reached an all-time low over here; you'll be
impressed. Are you passing Dunkin' Donuts on the way?"

Like anything else in life, there's just comfort in numbers, and
moms really need each other. Here's literally a recent text chain
between my mom BFF and me. Anyone relate?

Mom BFF: "OMG these kids have every toy in the world and
they've been fighting and screaming all day, I have such a headache.
Ahhhhhhhhh ... BRATS!!!!"

Me: "ugghghgh, so sorry. Eli just pooped his pants and we're in
line at Costco and I refuse to leave ... he doesn't have diaper on."

Mom BFF: "He just texted he's working late again, and I've been literally counting the seconds 'til 5. Tell me I'll be able to feel again."

Me: "I will, if you tell me what the sky looks like. Kenai's been sick since Tuesday—haven't left the house since."

People without kids feel this type of communication indicates weakness, dissatisfaction with life, or a complaining spirit. People with kids know that if you didn't have some form of outlet and friend to vent to, you'd start locking yourself in the bathroom again to Pilates breathe. "Mommy will be right out!" Exhaaaaale ...

And if you attempt to garner empathy from your non-mom friends, you're never met with the right reciprocity. They'll text things like "Oh, bad day? How are those little hams doing?" *Come get 'em and find out.* Describing parental woes to childless girlfriends is what I imagine it'd be like describing snow to Africans. They just cannot grasp the magnitude of the situation, so their responses and levels of compassion simply don't cut it.

Me: "Eli won't go back to sleep if he wakes up past 3. I make the Walking Dead look rested."

Childless friend: "Ugh, I KNOW, I've been going to bed so late I can barely wake up lately too. Can't you just put him back in the crib and turn the monitor off???"

Me: "I'm sorry I can't make it tonight, the kids are so crabby and I just know it'll be a disaster if I come."

Childless friend: "What?! No you have to come, they'll be fine. Just put Netflix on for them in my room!"

You don't know what makes you want to harm her more—the fact that she's guilting you into coming to her umpteenth Stella & Dot party this year, or the level of carefree ignorance leading her to believe your lunatic toddlers would stay put on a bed for two hours of purse-party goodness. There might be a better chance of the earth standing still.

But how could our friend know this? She still functions in the land of the living, enjoying hot food and Saturday morning yoga. We wish they knew how easy they have it but refrain from giving the full picture, for fear we'll permanently frighten them out of motherhood. But if we did, it might look something like this:

Dear childless friend,

I know you think you have problems now, that life is full of stress. Your roommate didn't pay her share of the Wi-Fi bill last month, and your thighs aren't adhering to the Paleo diet's promise. I am here to tell you: exhale. You have no problems. Your version of stress, aka frizzy hair and an increased insurance rate, are dilemmas you'll someday dream about. Don't be frightened, but it's true. Your version of a tough week, when your Amazon package came late despite your upgrade to Prime, is child's play compared to the gargantuan-sized plights you'll face post-kid. I'll trade an obnoxious Tinder exchange for a child refusing to ride the bus any day. Better you know what awaits so you can appreciate life as you know it.

Let's start with that negative body image. Stop complaining about your looks. Embrace whatcha got, my dear. Pampering and self-care will be reduced to an immeasurably small modicum of time, and there will be moments you hardly recognize yourself. I've recently gone shopping with hardened poop under my nail, and peed myself when laughing too hard. We won't even discuss the trampoline incident. You're not ready. Also, embrace your boobs, while you still have them. Stop hatin' on those nanoscale-sized works of wonder and celebrate all that is perky. They don't have bite marks, they won't leak without notice, and they don't hang south of the equator when you remove your socks.

You should also know how life's simple tasks, like getting ready to go out, or cooking a meal, will become Olympian feats worthy of a medal. For this reason, beware: never arrive late to a gathering attended by mom friends and claim it was "hard" getting out of the house. Be assured they will resent you with every word of explanation. They were childless once too and know that your lateness was a result of your nail color drying unpredictably slow and comparing pencil skirts in an online shopping vortex. Polish it up while you can, my dear, because leaving the house in the future will require you feeding four humans, extracting milk from your body, and sprinting down the driveway like an Olympian as your two-year-old screams, "MOOOOM, DON'T GOOOOOO!!!!" This nonsense can beat the buzz from the best of pinots, I assure you.

Another nugget of advice: treasure life's natural gifts, like sleep and food consumption. If all you do 'til the moment that egg is fertilized is achieve that pie in the sky known as REM, you won't regret it. This is what I'm telling you: Sleep, go to the movies, and eat hot food, slowly. Do not, however, speak of any superfluous amounts of slumber to aforementioned mom friends. Complaining with all seriousness that your dog woke you up at 9:30 a.m. on a Saturday will compromise the friendship, indefinitely.

And while not sleeping, savor the simple pleasures you might take for granted, despite all the distractions of your electrifying social life, yoga posing, and shoe shopping. Take baths for no reason whenever possible, while there's zero chance of someone bursting in to relieve themselves while explaining the intricacies of Lego Chima.

Yes, my solo friend, live it up before ya give it up. Blessings.

We're not jealous (that much), but the fact is, it can be a bit difficult remaining as close to your bestie when there's such a big part of your life she can't relate to. And vice versa. I'm sure my level of interest listening to her endless Match date fails is continually disappointing, as is my level of empathy when she complains about not having enough time for the gym. You don't want to become one of those moms, devaluing others' experiences because they haven't climbed the Everest of life and birthed a child, and you want to be there for them, even when you've literally had five hours of sleep … in two days.

Childless BFF: "Hey that movie's playing at 10 tonight, wanna go?"

Me: "Are you insane? I've been up since five."

Childless BFF: "Oh. Right."

And while your friendships with long-time besties change through motherhood, so ones form with others you never thought possible, just because you share the bond of motherhood. Once, a coworker and I mutually discovered we each had boys. We were totally opposite personalities and never said a word to each other in two years, but from the moment she overheard me talking about my run-in with a psychotic pediatric nurse, we've been close ever since.

"Oh my gosh, you have three kids?!"

"Yes, and I didn't know you did too! How are we alive?!"

Now we get lunch daily. When you discover someone in your life is a parent of small children, immediately you're bonded, like how I imagine veterans feel discovering each fought in 'Nam. You've both seen things no one else has, sunk to unthinkable lows, and survived pregnancy, birth, and the toddler years. You might as well take a blood oath.

Indeed, we need each other. And to help those still in search of a kindred, non-anal mom friend, here are some tips I've developed on my way out of Lonelyville:

Church is the best place to begin. The obvious start would be to join your church's MOPS group, but since mine seemed a bit intense (they actually wore MOPS T-shirts), I took the less intrusive route and stalked normal-looking moms in the café after service, even Facebook stalking before I made an introduction, to make sure they had a 50/50 ratio of personal posts to child photos and didn't upload only their children's quotable moments.

Join a midday life group, where moms will most likely attend. If your church doesn't have one, start your own at home or at the church, making it a kid-friendly moms' Bible study. "Children welcome" is the new "Snacks provided" when it comes to social recruitment.

The park or library: It's tempting not to throw on a baseball and be anti when you're makeup-less and sleep-deprived, but similar to dating, you'll never meet a mom friend if you don't try. You unfortunately might have to appear friendly, smile, make eye contact, and strike up convos when/if you ever spot a kindred soul. Like the old days of trying to meet a man, just smile, but don't look too desperate or needy, or they might pass you by. Just a cool, moderately intelligent chic, lookin' to make a friend, people.

Say yes to the blind dates, and ask for the digits. So many of my working friends would tell me about their "nice friends with kids the same age," who would be great mom friends but we'd never meet. They were like urban legends, like the couple that met comparing bananas in the produce aisle. Finally, I asked my friends to arrange a mommy date, as awkward as that sounded. But times get desperate when your only daytime companion is your cousin-turned-mom-friend by default. And if you hit it off with a new friend at the park or wherever, absolutely get their Facebook stats or give her your digits. There are four parks in my town, and very few moms who agree Crocs are the devil's footwear. "We really can't take chances. Here's my number. Text me if you want to meet here next week!"

CHAPTER 26

My Little Men

Sometimes I look around and wonder, do other families live like this? It's not so much the perpetual clutter and chaos but the overall circus that goes on behind closed doors. For one thing, I am surrounded by naked boys. I don't know when it began, but my kids are nude and they are proud. From the moment they step off the bus, there is a parade of flashing, mooning, and general pantlessness. And since they both refuse to wear underwear (choose your battles, man) their manhood can appear at any given moment. I've never thought male private parts were aesthetically pleasing, and now I'm offended by them, daily.

Our youngest has mastered the art of surprise in this arena, standing motionless from behind, to ensure the full shock of finding a wiener directly in your face. I can already feel the judgment of some, wondering why I would let my children shun undergarments and run amok in the nude, but I figure this is just a phase. Childhood innocence only lasts so long. If they're assailing furniture with their ding dongs at eleven, I'll revisit my position.

I'm sure coming from a family of sisters has something to do with my perpetual state of shock, but I would love to know if other male-dominated homes are as uncivilized. I know one friend who manages to keep her boys from jumping on couches, yelling, and running inside, period. She's either lying or herbally medicating her children. "PB & lavender-oil sandwiches, boys!" My house is the opposite—boys swinging from door hangings like tree-dwelling mandrills, flying from table to chair, and committing hourly acts of violence. Sometimes I'm envious of those friends who keep this barbarism at bay, but most times I think, eh, let 'em live. Our couches are crap anyway.

What disturbs me more is the boyish verbiage I'm constantly shocked by. There was a season I worried my youngest had a mild form of Tourette's, after he began inserting the word "butt" or "fart" into every other sentence. It was either send him to his room permanently, or tolerate such banter:

"Kenai, what do you want for lunch?"

"How 'bout poop sandwich, fart fart mama?"

"Kenai, what'd you do in gym today?"

"I played butt ball, hahaha! BUTT ball!"

"I said no more butt words. Go to your room."

"Hahaha, Mom said *butt*!"

This is your life living with Beavis and Butthead, without daughters. No hair braiding or nail-painting parties. Just endlessly yelling not to put the soap bar up their butt. No dancing to Princess Ariel's mermaid songs, just pillow fighting to the death and facing declarations of wrestling battles before you can knock off your stilettos. I sometimes wonder if other moms tap out at this point. Or are we all surrendering to a life of sword and pillow for three hours a night? I spent the entire winter of 2014 pretending to be a dragon that gets the stuffing kicked out of him by two defenders of the realm. There were bruises.

Battle wounds aside, having boys does have its perks. For one, they're less maintenance than girls. I've heard the stories. Five-year-old girls freaking out before school because they can't find the right headband, or a thirteen-year-old girl going on a hunger strike because she couldn't wear makeup. Parents of daughters are a testament to our race.

Because until teenagehood most boys don't give a hoot what they wear to school, or anywhere else for that matter. I've stopped my oldest from walking out the door with his shirt inside out and hair standing on end—and been met with disdain every time.

"Mom, it's FINE!"

"You look homeless. Get back inside."

Not a vain care in the world, like a bunch of cenobite monks. I save twenty bucks a month cutting their hair myself and can attest they've left the house some days looking like they ran headfirst into a lawn mower. No complaints. Kenai unknowingly rocked an uneven bowl cut for three years before a friend intervened on his behalf with a "how to cut hair" YouTube link.

But it wasn't until spending prolapsed amounts of time with my nieces and friends' daughters that I began to fully appreciate the simplicity of my boys, and most importantly, their ability to shut up. Never, ever have I had a longer, more torturous car ride than with a four-year-old girl abusing my ears with questions for an hour straight. I'm not sure she took a breath, and I was cross-eyed in head pain by the end of it. It was like being trapped in a prison cell with Rain Man. I've been head-butted, kicked in the "nuts" (yes, my children think I have a pair), and mistakably punched in the face, and I prefer such abuse over the mental exhaustion little girls bring. I tend to either shut down or get far too "real" for my sister's homeschooled kids after question number 109 from her twin ten-year-olds.

"Auntie, how come your car is so messy? Why don't you like to cook like Mom does? Why don't you want another baby?" *Because it could be a girl.* They're like walking, tablet-holding birth-control campaigns, and they're very effective. After watching them for an entire weekend, I made a gyno appointment to make sure my ParaGard was intact. That copper ring of goodness is supposed to stand firm for a decade, but we needn't take chances.

My boys might drain the energy out of me by 10:00 a.m., and turn me gray by thirty watching them jump, dive, run, and knee-scrape through the day, but I think there's a special bond that exists between mothers and our sons. They're our dudes. Our little men. Nothing compares to the feeling when they wrap their lil' arms around my neck, turn my chin toward their pudgy cheeks, and proclaim "Mom! I love you!" in those raspy voices. I sometimes picture what it will be like, with all three of them, grown tall and strong, coming to visit me when I'm old and— Never mind, not enough Kleenex.

Watching kids grow up must be what it's like for God watching us experience life's mysteries for the first time. They're like a tiny glimpse into God's heart. Their wild curiosity and explorative nature always amaze me. Everything—mixing cookie dough, washing the car, a walk through the yard—becomes a wild adventure with kids. They have a wide-eyed, enthusiastic approach to the world that makes everyday living magical. I think witnessing the unbridled enthusiasm of children is God's way of reminding us how phenomenal the world around us really is; the simple things like the way popcorn pops, the way grass smells after it rains, and—"Mom, look how big that pile of dog poo is"—okay, it's not all magic.

Children are gifts that allow us to relive some of the best parts of life. All we need is endurance, patience, and (at least for my kids) lots and lots of Band-Aids.

THIS IS WHY WE HAVE 'EM

CHAPTER 27

Stopping to Smell the Roses ... Even When They're Eating Them

My sister came over the other day, eyes as puffy as could be. She confessed in a shaky voice she had watched *Toy Story 3* the night before, and cried so uncontrollably she scared her children. Apparently the scenes with Andy leaving for college were too much for her. I mocked her sensitivity ... and then my oldest turned ten. I don't know what came over me, but it was utterly heartbreaking. The double digits just made it click: wait a minute, ten plus six is sixteen. In six years he'll be driving a car. Ten plus eight is eighteen. My baby will be leaving me in less time than he has been alive, and I still feel like he's five. Just writing this panics me.

I think mothers have different levels of attachments to their children. Some always look forward to the next stage in life, imagining their child's future and embracing change. Others like myself tend to cringe with every outgrown pant and inch grown, despite how difficult and challenging we find our current stage. Basically I've done everything in my power to keep my oldest from growing up. I didn't love every stage of having kids, but I also don't want them to get any older. I often find myself watching them play, wishing I could freeze them at the exact stage they're at. A bit creepy, but it calms me.

In fact, I think I developed borderline personality disorder the day Jack was born. It went beyond protectiveness. An hour post-birth, I dragged my half-paralyzed body to the nursery when the nurses didn't bring him to my room. There I was, teetering like a junkie; face smooched against the glass to make sure they knew I was all business. *Where is my baby?!* Whomever read my comment card that day got a memorable dose of crazy from room 27.

This nonsense didn't end once returning home. When a relative stopped by to take my precious infant on a "quick" stroller ride, I lost any grip on reality a solid thirty minutes later. *Where is she? Doesn't she know he'll be hungry? I am going to kill her!* I cringe writing this, but after forty-five minutes, I began imagining her trading him on the black market to fund a recreational drug habit. I might've canvassed the area in my car. Of course she shortly returned from this magical mystery ride, but that didn't stop me from getting all crazy cakes on a very unknowing, and might I mention very forgiving, kin.

Most similarly spirited first timers will agree: the instant you have a child, it's us against the world. Normal, seemingly innocent people are now outsiders who could potentially steal our baby, get them sick, or as they get older, demoralize them with bad media choices. I finally mustered up the strength to put Jack in our church nursery—the first time being left with "strangers." After waging death threats against an elderly nursery worker to make sure she paged me if he cried more than two minutes, I did well in my pew. For five minutes. Then the crazy kicked in, and unlike all the other God-fearing souls trusting the

Lord, I decided to spy on the nursery, on all fours, peeking through the door to make sure my no-cry rule was being upheld. *I know what these gals are up to. They're gonna let him cry thinking I need a break. Deceivers!* Sure enough my CIA instincts were correct, and I burst into the room, commandeering my wailing child and chastising gramma for ignoring my will. She was gracious, but there was fear in her eyes. They made me sign up for nursery duty the next week.

When I had to leave Jack at a home day care as a single mom, I wailed during my entire forty-minute commute and cried in the bathroom at least once a day. But all these moments pale in comparison to the moment that changed everything when he was eleven. I got the dreaded phone call at approximately 8:00 p.m. It was a close family friend, who was having Jack over that night. It went something like this: "Hey, we're doing Bible devotions and the boys just asked me what sexual immorality means. I'm going to give them the talk about sex and I didn't know if you want Jack to be part of it or not." I got light headed for moment and I think I mumbled incoherently, trying to gather my thoughts. I had fought tooth and nail for ten years to preserve my boy's innocence and this man wanted to tell him where his manhood went?! I rationalized with myself quickly that if I didn't let it happen now, he'd be sixteen thinking babies came from angel whispers. So with great hesitancy I said yes. I remember sitting in bed in tears that night: *my baby's innocence is lost forever.* It was tragic.

Thankfully he is still my Lego-playing little man, but having such an older child makes my clinginess with the younger two even worse. My fellow cling-on moms understand. I find myself staring at the kids' faces endlessly, just trying to soak up the moments. My rearview mirror is permanently affixed on the backseat so I can watch their little heads bob around in their car seat as we truck along. I just get crazy, thinking in twenty years these are the home movies I'll be sobbing over, watching their chubby legs run and chipmunk voices sing.

It hits us constantly. As much as we complain about the insanity of having young children, the thought that one day our babies will be gone is so scary. Yes, they'll be the same people, but their little faces and personalities will change *forever*. I think I scared the life out of my husband one night during a hormonal bout of panic: "Honey, you think you'll remember them like this, but you never do and then they grow up and they're *gone!*" Poor guy must have taped four hours of video the next day.

Motherhood is mind-numbingly tough, but we still want to take it all in and know we cherished the moments we had. I haven't mastered a ton of maternal skills, but God has given me a strong ability to appreciate, *really* appreciate, simple moments with my kids on a daily basis. It's such a good way to live, realizing every day is truly a gift and a chance to be better, more joyful, and more grateful. I think experiencing loss at a young age helps me live with a heightened awareness of how precious, and even fragile, life is. Those moments watching my boys pick dandelions—"*Danderwions*, Mom!"—and placing them in my hair make up for the fact that one of them secretly ate the first handful. Hearing their little voices laughing hysterically from their bunk beds at night. Pushing them on the swings when Eli put his hands behind his head and said with a sigh, "Life is good, Mom ..."

"It really is, buddy." *Sniff.*

CHAPTER 28

Things I Said I'd Never Do ... and Then I Had Kids

As with most first-time mothers, I was shocked at how much love I felt, from the second my son was born. With Jack, my first, I physically sensed all the hardness of heart and heaviness of "self" melting away through some sick phenomenon that made me cry for two days straight. You finally get it. The miracle of life isn't just physical; it's emotional. The supernatural ability to love so powerfully and unconditionally is probably what began turning my heart toward God. How else could it be explained?

This is why your friends lose their minds watching their kids perform in a school play, and why your coworkers won't shut up about their baby's "amazing" motor skills. This is why people litter their cubes with ugly kid art and buy minivans without feeling their humanity has been violated. Now your entire focus is making this tiny human happy. Like the most generic Hallmark card known to man. But it's true. One look at that newborn transforms you into a Hoover, snuffing away at their heads and practically eating their cheeks. I literally salivated for my baby when I saw him after being apart. Not even sure what to say there, but it's all shock for the former narcissist.

The downside of all this beauty is that, instantly, you become "that parent," acting a fool out of blind love, and speaking in horrible generalizations: "I can't believe how much I love him! I think he's the cutest child I've ever seen." You live with your thumb hovering over the record button, ready to capture baby magic at any moment, and Facebook post every moment. You've become the parent who says, "Good job!" and "That's *so* great, honey," after your kid dots an *i*. "No skid marks today, sweetie? You're a rock star!" One fully formed circle and clearly your kid's a prodigy.

I first realized I could not be trusted after lashing out at a friend who joked about my newborn's big ears. I basically transformed into Dumbo's mother and unleashed for two minutes before regaining control. You just can't take the thought of someone hurting or making fun of your kid, and when it happens—such as a kid pushing your toddler on the playground—it's over. *Okay, freckles, you're goin' down.* I don't care if you're an MIT scholar with the temperament of Jesus, you will lose your senses for the sake of your kid, at least once. You'll ask for rules to be bent, apologies to be made, and maybe even tell the neighbor to shut his dog up so your baby can nap. Cringe-worthy, humiliating behavior you never thought you were capable of, pre-kid.

My worse offense thus far has been writing a letter to my child's teacher and cc-ing the principal, asking if my son could still receive a "pride of the school" trophy, even though he had received more than the allowed number of tallies. This desperate

pitch became a two-page manifesto, relaying how my bad parenting habits of not signing homework caused this trophy injustice,
and could she please bend the rules this once. This was her exact
response:

Dear Mrs. Kastner,

I'm not sure why your son told you he's not getting a trophy. He
is slated to receive a Pride of CCA trophy with the rest of the class
during the presentation. I hope this helps.

Note to irrational self: before divulging your clear issues to school
leadership, make sure information relayed by someone who refuses
to wear underwear is indeed accurate. *Someone shoot me.*

Really, it's like mad cow disease. You lose the ability to assess clearly
and rationalize, and you slowly transmute into an overemotional, less
couth version of yourself.

Of course all this insanity and abandonment of pride
stems from complete love, but I find some parental "lows" to
be particularly egregious, as we find ourselves doing things we
never imagined possible, pre-kid. Like most parental delusions,
many of us imagined offering our broods organic baby food fresh
from the juicer each morn, then progressing to a diet of whole
grains, veggies, and an overall preservative-free fantasy. However,
somewhere between toddlerhood and preschool, your kid just
might develop a distaste for practically all nutritious food with the
exception of grilled cheese, sauce-free pizza, and oddly enough,
edamame. At first you resist this senseless food strike—what kind
of kid doesn't like strawberries?—but after months of experiments,

artful persuasions, and bribes, dinnertime becomes a battlefield of the wills no parent is armed for. "So, guys, what was the best part of your— SWALLOW that carrot right now! CHEW!"

For those of us who hate cooking, it's bad enough schlepping over a stove each night, even for grateful patrons. This mediocre lasagna didn't bake itself, people: buckle up. But after years of closed-mouthed resistance, many of us weaken and find ourselves in the fluorescently lit shame of our frozen foods section, staring at a bag of dino nuggets and wondering if we can really feed our children glamourized entrails. If you're desperate enough, the answer to this nutritional quandary is yes. Yes, you can. And before you know it, your cart is brimming with red no. 40 and hydrogenated corn oil, steamrolling past the organic produce section in avoidance of self-judgment. All of which you'll serve that night with a multivitamin and a smile on your face. Dinnertime, guys!

Another parental pitfall I've sunk into comes in the arena of social media. Before shedding my inner Luddite and joining Facebook, I would sit in sheer amazement at my mom friends' clear loss of senses. Posting photos of your kids' milestones, accomplishments, and especially cute moments is acceptable, of course. If lil' Aiden got a Cub Scouts award, then darnit, the world should know about it. What I could not comprehend, however, were parents who posted their child's every waking moment on the World Wide Web. Ten consecutive pictures of your one-year-old sleeping is not a FB update; it's an abuse of technology.

But alas, I've found myself guilty of this annoying habit, to a degree. It's just so tempting, when gazing at your child's perfect chubby cheeks—*Now this is definitely post material.* I've slowly become the parent I swore I'd never be, trolling after my kids through the park with my thumb hovering over "record" like the paparazzi following Kim K. "One more time down the slide, looking at Mommy this time!" But, parents-to-be, know this: No one. Not your bestie, not your closest coworker, and most certainly no one on your Twitter feed gives a flying monkey about your kid's letter recognition skills or a photo montage of them napping. It's only through hindsight that I gain this insight and self-awareness. Your judgment is clouded by fecal fumes and first-time-parent delusion. Trust.

But none of these shocking parental behaviors comes close to the transformation experienced in the realm of sports. When my children were babies, I prayed many blessings over their lives. A close relationship with God, health, and of course that they would be saved from the brain-cell-sucking vortex that is organized sports. Growing up in a die-hard football town, I've seen what idolizing pig leather can do for the ego, and the IQ. So when Kenai came home from kindergarten with a flag football slip from school, I did what any other protective mother would do—shoved it in the Dumpster. Demanding vaccines was one thing, but no way was the public school system gonna brainwash my baby into a jock at age five.

But as fate would have it, another parental plan was crushed and we eventually found ourselves on the sidelines of the Blue Knights field every Saturday at 9:00 a.m. with all the other Kool-Aid drinkers hoping they'd spawned the next Manning.

What happened within a few weeks, however, I can't explain. It was all over at Kenai's first attempt at a touchdown. There I was, running down the yard lines, yelling and cheering like Mike Ditka himself. I was addicted. Sure, he'd fallen flat on his face and run the wrong direction, but clearly, my kid had Super Bowl victory in his genes. I have a feeling I'll be working concession stands and screaming things like "We bleed Blue!" in the future, but I figure two outta three answered prayers isn't bad.

CHAPTER 29

For the Single Mommies: Well, at Least You Chose Life

This chapter's title might sound awful, but when I feel like a failure with Jack, especially during the years I was solo parenting, I honestly told myself: "Well, at least he's alive." Is there any way to capture in words the special sort of madness beheld solely by the single parent? Man or woman, this is an experience separating the men from the boys. Shout out to all those holdin' down the circus that is single parenthood. Whether choosing single parenthood or on an unplanned journey, this is where it gets real. How real, one might wonder? Oh, say, as real as driving your colicky infant around, pulling into random cul-de-sacs, and calmly exiting the car only to scream into the night air. Repeat if necessary, because baby daddy ain't here for second shift. I burnt fuel I couldn't afford for three months straight, literally pinching myself to stay awake on the road to get my screaming child to sleep. It gets as real as never, ever buying good clothes again (okay, any clothes) to foot the day-care bill, or taking your son to "Touch-a-Truck" and other man-based activities after he began using his wrench as an eyelash curler.

The challenges and special moments of single parenthood could never be summed up in a chapter. The love you exude and receive by being a sole parent is indescribable. The flip side is you never have enough time and energy, so you feel like you're never doing enough. Everyone calls you a hero, but you feel like the wack job they cast in every reality show so everybody feels better about themselves.

But of all challenges and crazy experiences found in single mommihood, dating has got to be one of the most memorable. Ah, the joy of trying to appear free spirited and fun and score a good man when you're a baby mama. The elation of that moment a guy's smile fades when he spots a baby carrier in your backseat. "What is that?!" *It's a car seat, not an MK 20, jerko.* The blissful call, mid-date, that your kid's puking buckets. That shrieking cry from the crib juuuust when he's about to say the *l* word. The list goes on, but all tales of courting glory are dwarfed by the worst date experience in my seven-year foray as a single mom.

A first-time suitor picked me up one fine eve, and the stars appeared to be aligning. My mom was there to ensure a smooth departure with Jack. The man was taller than described, and he didn't seem phased by having to step over a child gate upon entry. My escape was about to play out with unprecedented smoothness—until Jack's arm became lodged in between a chair rod and all the horses in hades broke loose. We're talking the mother of all meltdown kind of screaming that nothing could have prepared this brave bachelor for. I was not surprised by the look on his face, or the lack of shock when there was no date number two.

And then when the date becomes a boyfriend, and has to interact with your kid, there will be awkwardness beyond measure. Not the rookie-level embarrassment you experienced dating while childless, when just a zit or bad hair day was something to fret about. We're talking the kind of humiliation felt after your two-year-old tells the man of your dreams his mommy made a funny bubble when she farted in the bath. Or the kind of shame that ensued when your toddler has a total fit in a restaurant, and you have to remain cool, stern, and of course cute, as you high-heel his butt to the bathroom for a spanking.

Dating with kids is especially fun when you're the type of lady who wants everything perfect, for at least six months of delusion. Lip gloss gleaming and perfect hair slightly tousled to appear casual before the doorbell rings. House deceitfully clean before every visit, and outfit envisioned before every outing. This sociopathic behavior becomes unhinged, of course, while raising a man-child that demands you sing *Veggie Tales* a capella style to your date upon arrival. Or when your little one proudly announces his "nuts are itchy" and inquires as to whether your date's nuts are in fact just as itchy. Awesome stuff.

All we want to do is find a man who loves God, loves our kid, and has an immeasurable tolerance for butt jokes. No, there's nothing easy or very sexy about dating as a single mama, but we make it work, one pair of Spanx at a time. And understanding it can't be easy dating a single mom for the first time, I've developed this bullet list of tips for incoming suitors, to improve the outcome:

- Please don't call our kid "buddy" or "sweetheart" upon meeting. It's tacky, and confusing, since the last three suitors aren't our buddies anymore.

- Please don't wrestle or attempt physical contact without knowing our kids first. We've seen too many predator episodes on *Dateline*.

- Please don't refer to my child as the "icing on the cake." I'm not a pastry, and you're totally lying. That's a sin.

- When my kid does something awful in public, or says something to humiliate me (e.g., fart bubbles), look away, pretend you didn't notice, or leave the room if necessary.

- Don't correct or instruct my kid before we're close to engagement. I got this far without parent B's opinion, and I'll be reactivating my Christian Mingle account tomorrow if you don't knock it off.

- Don't ever talk about having kids of our own someday, at least 'til ya put a ring on it. I got four hours of sleep last night. Back it up.

- Please don't ever comment that we "look hot, for having children." This is like saying you're smart, for a man.

ENOUGH OF THIS FOOLISHNESS ... BRING ON THE TAKEAWAYS!

CHAPTER 30

Don't Forget Your Prayer Closet

I think what makes the best kids is the best you. At the risk of sounding all Joel Osteen, I believe the number one way to be your "best self" is by remaining close to God. You + God = happy mama, and everyone—the hubs, the kids, and the snarky school secretary you almost assaulted during last month's estrogen surge—really does agree.

Whenever friends share about being frustrated at home (or anywhere, really), I always ask how their prayer time has been. Especially moms with young babies, because it's so hard to find a quiet anything, let alone an actual sliver of time spent in the Word and prayer. After my lady parts underwent the irreversible blunt trauma of birthing two babies in less than two years, I went without dedicated quiet time for years. Sure, you pray during the biweekly shower, or in the car when your thoughts aren't massacred by Wiggles songs, but without personal time with God, it's rough. Looking back, I wonder if I consider those early years the hardest because I wasn't a baby person, or I wasn't spending enough time with the Lord.

It makes total sense—when you're with God, you manifest his characteristics—patience, long-suffering, kindness—did I mention long-suffering? And you'll be much more equipped to handle your two-year-old dispersing fireplace ash around the carpet or your son telling you his waterfowl report is due tomorrow. And he needs pictures. And the printer's out of ink. At times like these, "I can do all things through Christ who strengthens me" translates to not crashing your car in fury while driving to Staples for HP tricolor economy ink. That quiet-time dose of 2 Peter might just have saved you.

I can't even imagine my pre-Christian self as a mother. Seriously, more than the mystery of how Kim Kardashian has become a societal icon, I don't know how parents do it without the Lord. I'm the salt of the earth and a light on some sort of hill, and I can barely get through some days. But if I'm honest with myself, there is a direct correlation to the amount of peace in my home and joy in my spirit, with the amount and quality of alone time with the Lord.

It's so easy to convince ourselves that we're spiritually mature enough to make it days, even weeks, without being in the Word and prayer. Just another crafty lie from the enemy that affects our kids and our home life more than anything. Reserving alone time for God can seem nearly impossible when you're sleep-deprived with an infant, or working full time, but it's just worth it. We might have been awake at 5:00, and the house clutter could pass for an ADT security billboard (Don't let home invasion happen to you!), but God still wants us to make time for him, for our own good.

I used to think because I'm home with the kids, in a safe, Christ-dwelling place, that the Ephesians 6 warning to put on the whole armor of God was less relevant. It's not like I'm out there fighting

evil in a corrupt workplace or being influenced in the worldly atmo-
spheres I used to face. Lie from the enemy. Sometimes when we're
home, and isolated, feeling defeated and strained, the worst attacks
can happen. And the consequences are more lethal, because they'll
affect our children and our marriage.

Ten minutes with God every day not only protects our hearts
from defeat, but God usually multiplies your time and your energy
as a reward for putting him first when you had none. One time I
prayed silently at 6:00 a.m. because my lips were too tired to move,
asking for energy and grace for school shopping with toddlers in
tow. Three hours later a friend showed up at my doorstep with a
surprise venti pumpkin latte saying her remodelers had commandeered her house and asking if she could hang with the kids while I
shopped. I have been gifted with many joyous moments in life, but
I swear that made top ten. If I were an Israelite seeing manna drop
out of the sky for the first time, I would have felt less awe. God is
always faithful.

The single greatest blessing in my life is having healthy, kind-
hearted kids, and I take zero credit. If anything, someone like me
procreating should have done the world a disservice, but since I've
been saved, God has given me a constant sense of joy and peace that
I attribute to the great boys I've been able to raise (so far … still
praying). Our kids are a direct product of the environment we create
at home. If we have a worshipful spirit and our hearts are centered
on God, they're going to benefit. You rarely come across a total terror
of a child whose parents are true Christians, operating in the fruit of
the Spirit ("We don't know what happened. All of a sudden we were
having home church and he started dropping the f-bomb!").

No matter what our home circumstances look like, no matter how many kids we have, if we keep our relationship with him front and center, we'll be much happier moms, and our kids will turn out great. Don't forget to access the power God's waiting to give, and don't feel guilty for asking God for patience by the hour. I called down the heavens once during a second hour of Play-Doh time—Jesus, take the wheel.

CHAPTER 31

Motherhood, Your Art Form

When I get to heaven, I will have two questions for the Lord. The first is the common query of why innocents had to suffer on earth. The other would be why he mistakenly forgot to bequeath me with the talent and body frame necessary to be a contemporary dancer, when it was my heart's desire for so long. Of course that ship sailed decades ago, but during my delusional habit of pretending to be a "pointe" dancer while squatting to episodes of *So You Think You Can Dance*, I had a deep revelation about motherhood. A contestant said, "Dancing is not about technicality; it's about your individuality, and when you're doing what you love, the audience loves it, you feel alive, you stop critiquing and enjoy the dance." I sat there thinking, I sure wish motherhood could be the same way.

Because really, motherhood is an art form. Your kids are your canvas, and there's no right or certain way to mother. This kind of freeness can feel scary at first, but the longer you're a mom, the more you learn to craft your own style and approach parenthood in a way that suits your personality, and your kids' needs. I think new moms and even some of us veterans get tripped up by feeling our home life has to look a certain way based on our childhood memories, delusions of grandeur, or comparison to friends. But since no child, mother, or set of circumstances are exactly the same, and since nothing (sweet Moses, nothing) prepares us for motherhood, we'll never have it all "right." And just like any form of art, imitation stinks.

I used to feel bad that dinnertime in my house was such a clear disaster, especially compared to the five-star meals I remember from childhood, beginning with us all running like cheetahs to devour some homemade scrumptiousness, and ending with my dad declaring, "Good meal, hun!" So when my dinners consistently looked like a scene from *Gremlins* and my husband purposely "missed" suppertime to avoid the wreckage, I felt like such a failure. We all feel disappointment like this, whether it's feeling guilty when we dread helping with the kids' homework or when our family devotion time is about as Spirit filled as an Amish potluck.

But we need to get out of this habit, and here's why: comparing our family life to others', and always focusing on our limits or weaknesses, robs us of our joy. My childhood meals were great because my mom was home, and we owned a grocery store, for goodness sake. Free food and free time equal filet mignon Monday. She was a great mom, but I can't really remember her running around outside with us, or playing when we asked her to. That wasn't her thing. But it's mine, and it's what I feel my kids need most from me, at least in this phase of parenthood. So I've learned to let things go—I mean, really hand my feelings of inadequacy to the Lord and rejoice in what makes me a great mom.

Over time, I've learned to be thankful and proud of the ways God's allowed me to rock it as a mom. We should always pray for our weakness to improve, but appreciate the good in the meantime. Just like any other form of expression, the way you show love to your kids and your home life should be all your own. Then, like dancing, your audience—your family—will love it, you'll feel more alive, you'll stop critiquing and enjoy this season tenfold. Motherhood is the most beautiful expression of love, and kids are our ultimate creative product.

I'm a huge nurture-over-nature person. The way we act, what we teach, and how we interact with our kids shape the people they become. If we're always worried about doing things a certain way, or appearing as we think we should, it takes our focus off our kids and turns motherhood into a duty instead of an adventure.

I have homeschooling friends whose lack of home structure would horrify some type-A pals living on a block schedule ("Oh boy, it's 10:17, kids; time to color!"). No, these free-spirited moms let their kids choose their own lessons plans, stay up 'til 11:00 p.m., and eat on the floor, Indian style. They've been criticized, but their kids seem well adjusted and they sure look well rested when they wake at 10:00 a.m.

Tips for Becoming Your Own Mother Artist:

- Avoid self-imposed "rules" that aren't important. Don't feel you have to do the dishes before playing with your kids, or heck, even the next day. If your kid won't eat, buy a Ninja blender, make a smoothie with kale, and call it dinner, every night.

- Don't overschedule or overcommit: If you feel you've done too much running around and the kids don't want to go out, even when the weather's nice, then let go of your plans, throw the packed lunches back in the fridge, and just enjoy the day together. Anyone who's forced their kids to go on a playdate or "fun outing" has learned the hard way it's better to stay in and risk personal boredom. I'll take comfy sweats and Candy Land over tantrums in the library any day.

- Identify some things you really want your kids to experience and appreciate, and work them into your life. For me, that's nature. I don't care how late it is, if I spot a harvest moon out and they've already gone to bed, they're getting up anyway. No rules. I want them to know that even though life has structure and Mom wants them in bed, sometimes you have to break out and celebrate God's truly wondrous world. By being an appreciative person, you're going to create appreciative kids.

- Live in the moment. As much "The Power of Now's" message makes my blood boil, there's truth to understanding how to live in the moment, especially when you have young kids. Even when I feel like I might self-implode if being forced to play Super Smash Bros. just one more time, I've learned to concentrate on the beauty of the moment—watching their animated faces and hilarious commentary—instead of the fact that I just want to boil spaghetti. One of my sons used to take five minutes reading a single homework page while holding my eyelids open each night, but I discovered if I just focused on the way he formed his words, with his occasional lisp that I secretly loved, I found sweetness in the moment.

Some of us might be more Salvador Dali than Norman Rockwell, but motherhood is meant to be personal, creative, and expressive. Our kids are our canvas, the ultimate way we make our marks on the world. Anyway, the best artists have been known to be unorthodox, messy, and unorganized. *These kids are going to be flipping prodigies.*

CHAPTER 32

Our Crowns in Heaven Just Might Be Made of Plastic

Motherhood is a life choice and a lifestyle, but we often don't consider it a *job*. Describing motherhood as a duty sounds so loveless, and obligatory, but when you think about it, if we're blessed enough to have a child, raising kids is really our number one commission for this season of life. It sounds intimidating and overwhelming when you realize what a huge responsibility it is to raise a family, but it also helps prioritize life and get us through the more mundane, unpleasant tasks and experiences motherhood brings.

No matter what my work, friends, or personal interests demand of me, when I stick to the mantra that my kids really should come first, I'm a better mom and enjoy my kids more, especially when asked to play Power Rangers for the third time before dinner. Moms with any child over the age of one year have sat in the light of two truths: if you'd like to prevent your family from hearing your phone convo about vaginal irritation, turn off the baby monitor; and second, pretend play is the new colic. It can be sheer torture. I have a friend who recently paid her daughter $20 to get out of playing

Barbies after making a promise she just couldn't handle. For others, mommy martyrdom means saying yes when both kids want you to sing them to sleep and you still haven't scrubbed a single dinner dish. Are any mothers out there remaining conscious by stanza 17 of "This Little Light"? I'm shocked my children don't have night terrors after hearing me sleepily slur "Shesus lovesmeee … thish I know… zzzzz" like a drunk fighting a blackout. Other moms out there cringe at the mere hint of studying or homework, especially with younger kids that take fifteen minutes to write an eight-word sentence.

Saying yes when our kids want quality time, help, or even just attention can be so difficult, especially when it feels like we're being pulled in a million different directions, with so many things to do before the end of the day. But I really believe we'll regret not spending that time. People are living to ninety these days, and our kids will only need us for so long. The job, the social life, even the ministry will still be there in five years. But our kids might not be asking to cuddle or watch a movie then, and I've learned that more than good meals, more than our wallets, our kids need the most "present" form of us.

This approach to motherhood can actually be freeing, because if we get in the habit of not putting down our phones, or doing a puzzle despite the castle-sized pile of laundry in the corner, the temptation to say yes to distractions or self-imposed duties eventually decreases. The key is to train ourselves to operate this way daily and then figure out how to balance putting your kids first without losing yourself in the process.

I'm kind of anti-child-centric, in that I don't think parents should live under the thumb of a child who calls himself Captain Poop. Adults should still be the decision makers, not living at the whim of our kids, and I think it's vital to maintain healthy personal lives as long as our kids aren't paying the price. Many of us need to work and spend time sowing into our marriages and do personal activities we love; so we have to find a balance. Kind of like when you become a Christian: you learn how to put God first in your life without neglecting other important areas of life.

God comes first, then marriage, kids, etc., and it really boils down to putting your kids before yourself. Painful pretend play. Putting down the phone even after you uploaded the most magical photo and you *know* you've got at least forty likes. If you're single or divorced, that means resisting the urge to check your Christian Mingle account 'til that sweet post-bedtime hour. It means reading the devotional at dinner when you feel you'll burst a blood vessel if you don't check your email. *Just. One. Click.* Work will always be there. The gym can wait, and the laundry will eventually get folded (okay, I wrote that because I think that's what responsible mothers worry about). Our kids will be running out the door, ditching us for their friends before we know it. My advice: sword fight until the lightsaber dims, sing the *Frozen* songs until you're borderline deaf, and try to absorb every silly, sleep-deprived moment. It's always, always worth it. Amen. Let's stand.

Advice for Painful Self-Sacrificing Activities:

> - Go all in. It sounds like some MSNBC show hosted by an unstable liberal, but the idea here is committing to whatever activity you're dreading, to avoid being a half-hearted player. Otherwise it's like going on a date when your hubs would rather be watching the game. You can tell the difference

and so can your kids. If you're gonna join Scout Pack #40, it helps to be totally into it. Look at that stellar neckerchief. Like that adage "If you want to be happy, pretend you are."

- Set a mental time limit. Everything's easier when you can see, or at least know, the general direction of the light. Being Obi-Wan for forty minutes is an easier task to swallow when you know you revert back to human at 2:00 p.m.

- If you have to say no when your kids want you to play, because you just started a new butt workout that you just know will bring sexy back, give them an I-owe-you. They should know they're important, but you shouldn't have to drop everything at your kids' whims, and they need to know you have your own activities. I-owe-yous prevent you from being the bitter mommy schlepping to the petting zoo, again, against her will.

- When you're really strugglin', think "big picture." We live in a world where there are tangible results for everything: Exercise and look better. Work hard and get a paycheck. But there are no visible results or rewards found for spending quality time and being present for your kids. It seems like no one notices, but your kids' hearts do. Even if they don't express appreciation or seem to care about your sacrifices, your reward might just be in heaven, because God cares when we put our self aside for their good. Many, many crowns …

CHAPTER 33

Your Gorgeous Gut

My clear fail at the rhythm method may have led to three accidental pregnancies, but since God has a plan for each of us, I believe he gives each mom the keen ability to know what's best for her. There are very few powers in this world as instinctive as a mother's intuition. This isn't just an old wives' tale or some maternal superpower we use to justify worrying. It's the God-given ability to be in tune with your kids and to know when something's "off" or just needs attention. I've learned through the years if you sense something is wrong, there probably is.

Learning to trust your maternal instincts, even against the influence of other parents or friends, comes in time. I remember two friends getting into an argument around the campfire because one thought the other should be sharing "eternal truths" with their kids—the reality of hell and the consequences of sin, etc. My friend didn't back down, because she knew how sensitive her kids were, and what they could handle at the age of four. *Sorry, dude, my kid's scared of his goldfish. If you want to explain perpetual burning and sleep with him 'til he's ten ...*

Trusting your gut manifests in a lot of ways: not letting them sleep over at a friend's house whom you don't know well, even though all your other Christian friends gave the okay. Sensing something's bothering your kid, you sacrifice your solo shopping trip and take him along so he'll open up. Sensing there's a deeper reason your six-year-old suddenly never wants to be alone. Noticing your teen's been spending *way* too much time alone recently. In every case, it's tempting and easy to just brush off these sometimes slight observances or just chalk them up to over-worrying. But when you get a sense that there's more to the story, or something's just not "right" with your kid, it most likely isn't. You just have to make a habit of listening to your gut, which is really just God working through the maternal instinct he put there to begin with.

Recently, I was all set for my after-dinner jog, and Jack was still sitting at the dinner table. I felt bad leaving him alone, so although inwardly begrudging, I sat and made small talk. I remember my gut sensing he wanted to talk and feeling I shouldn't leave him alone. What followed was an hour-long chat about how he thought he was ready for public school and how he felt he was spiritually strong enough to handle it. That was a huge change for our family, after ten years of Christian schooling, and I'm not sure he would have ever brought it up if I hadn't made myself available and mustered through the twenty minutes of small talk and yes-and-no answers all mothers of boys endure.

There've been so many examples where mom friends of mine just knew, despite what doctors, friends, colleagues, and family members said, that they were right to pay attention to something going on with their children. Years ago, my sister was being told her son had emotional problems or ADD, when, after much research and a visit to an amazing homeopathic doctor, she discovered he had an allergy to red dye #40, which brings on tantrums and meltdowns. She just knew it had to be something other than what the world was telling her.

A big part of trusting your gut has to do with spending quality daily time with the kids, where actual conversations take place. Not assuming school or their playdate was fine, but really connecting with their hearts and making sure you're paying attention to what they're saying and feeling, despite the perpetual race to get through dinner, homework, practice, bath, and bed. If we're not "present" with our kids, we won't be in tune with our intuitions, because we won't notice. It's so easy to just assume everything's peachy with our kids—I mean, they wake, play, learn, eat; what else is there?—but we can forget there's still a lot going on in their hearts and minds, as they're continually adjusting and reacting to the new world around them, a lot of which we might not realize or know about.

Good counsel and professionals are a blessing and serve a great purpose. But we should never ignore these great guts.

CHAPTER 34

Let It Go

Let it go. Easier said than done for my type-A sistas, I know. But trying to control every part of your day or schedule when the kids are small is like walking into a hurricane and expecting your hair to stay salon smooth. You seriously cannot be a control freak and a happy mama at the same time.

Admittedly I don't have control issues. My neurosis tends to lie on the other side of the spectrum, where denial has its way. Bills can pile up, deadlines can loom, and I think, eh, Jesus could come back tomorrow. Worry not, thy heart.

While neither extreme lifestyle is healthy, I do think there's a helpful approach to how we balance our "plans" without letting our schedules dictate our lives.

For stay-at-homers especially, it can be hard not filling the calendar with playdates, outings, and planned activities to feel less lonely and break up the day. For me, I would schedule self-imposed activities—"C'mon, guys, we gotta be at the park/mall/library by eleven!"—and then get bent out of shape when a nap came on early or the boys didn't want to stop playing when it was time to go. Convincing ourselves we have to be somewhere when really no one would notice if we were raptured for the next eight hours, or constantly cleaning the house in total denial that no one except the cats will notice, can be comforting and help us have some sense of structure to the day. But sometimes we can get too caught up in keeping everything perfect, or hurrying from point A to B, and lose our ability to just pay attention and enjoy our kids.

It sounds corny and generic to "treasure every moment because they grow up so fast," but it's true. One of my biggest fears is regretting I spent more time worrying about things that didn't matter and rushing through my kids' younger years without really embracing the simple experiences and moments. The obvious solution is to avoid talking, texting, and uploading all day, but it goes way beyond that. It's less rushing our kids from car, to store, to house, to next activity—many times for no reason. Instead of walking at their pace, listening to their slow toddler babble, or waiting until they're done talking before interrupting to answer a two-minute-long question formation, we often just push them along, trying to meld them into our action-packed day, when really, they just need someone to sit on the floor and spend time with them. Just sit still, and *be*.

Of course there are certain things we have to get done, and we can't let the kids dictate where, when, and how we spend the day, but we really do need to "let it go," when it comes to thinking the house has to be in a certain condition and our lives to go according to plan on a daily basis. My friend recently admitted she's afraid her son's unhealthy perfectionism might stem from her type-A need to have every corner of her house remain orderly and spotless through his childhood, which many times overtook her joy as a new mom.

Yelling at your two-year-old for climbing up the covers because the bed is made, or refusing to play because you haven't vacuumed yet, kills our joy, and the belief that we can have control in our lives is a lie from the enemy giving us a false sense of security and a big time and energy suck from the people and things that should be our priorities.

Plan and accomplish what you need to, but try to relax about the rest. If your three-year-old wearing a new sweater just landed in a pile of mud on the way to a playdate, don't let it ruin your mood. Like it or not, in the land of parenthood, nothing is ever, ever going to be perfect or according to all the maternal fantasies that've been planted, watered, and dancing around our heads for a decade.

When the kids just want to stay in their jammies after you've envisioned an epic library day, or they just absolutely refuse to get wet after you've paid $50 admission to a water park, think "big picture." In the span of life, or really, even a week, these are not big deals, and it's easier to just go with it than insist on getting your own way ("you *will* swim in this wade pool!") or letting it ruin your entire day.

Cherishing the moments doesn't mean pretending to enjoy diaper changing, or relishing the fifteenth time you've had to make a potty-training pit stop. It's embracing the good moments that are there for the taking, like watching their faces in the rearview mirror or pausing to eavesdrop on the kids talking to each other in the bunk beds at night. Because scary as it is, we just don't know how many moments we'll have in life.

As hard as it was losing my dad, I can see, in God's sovereignty, how God has blessed me because of that void. He gave me an ability to live in the moment and appreciate what matters. You realize every day is a chance to make memories. I'm always thinking, not in a fearful way, but in a deeply appreciative way, this is a day I'll never get back, at a time in their lives I'll think about someday, wishing I could see those smiles and hear those little voices, just one more time. We're not going to be thinking about the coffee we didn't get to grab, or the workouts we missed because one kid's naptime didn't cooperate. I've ever so slowly learned to let go of what doesn't matter, to make room for what does.

CHAPTER 35

If It Ain't Broke ...

In the same way we sometimes compare ourselves to each other, I feel we do the same with our kids, sometimes expecting them to be more of what we expected or wanted them to be like. Whether wanting our kids to be more athletic, more academic, or just more like us, it can be hard when we don't totally jibe with our kids' interests or even their personalities as they get older. While it's our job to raise them in ways we see fit, and offer them every opportunity possible to develop, we also have to recognize, accept, and nurture the very unique people God created them to be—despite our own desires.

I remember thinking if I ever had kids, they'd be girls, and they'd be just like me. I only had sisters growing up, and I'm the spitting image of my mother, so why wouldn't the cycle perpetuate? I feel God can't even resist the temptation to mess with this kind of thinking. So three irreplaceable boys later, I'm left with an artsy introvert, an analytical overthinker, and an adrenaline junkie. If I hadn't witnessed their births myself, I'd wonder if they were even my kin.

And when our kids' interests are far from ours—"No piano lessons, guys, you sure?"—and there's not much we share in common as they get older, we can sometimes feel alienated from our own kids.

And it can be disappointing when our son or daughter refuses to play a sport or get involved in something we know they'd excel at and probably end up loving.

My oldest was the size of a spruce pine by fourth grade, leading friends, family, and even strangers to ask him constantly if he was his school's basketball star. Truth is, he tried, and he was just so very awful. Despite his gargantuan stature, he was petrified of contact sports, seen from his tee ball years when he'd spot a fly ball and flee like he was outrunning an avalanche. Basketball was a bit more painful, however, as he was three heads taller than his teammates and still could not make a single … blessed … shot.

I remember my very competitive uncle pressuring him, "You can't give up; ya gotta just practice more, sign up for camp," blah, blah, blah, but his heart just wasn't in it. He'd rather be making Minecraft villages worthy of the *Architectural Review* award, so he's never revisited the court. I never wanted him to feel bad about who he was, and I didn't want to become like so many parents trying to transfer their own dreams onto their kids, even competing with each other about their children's accomplishments. That's the worst flavor of Kool-Aid out there.

I think one of the coolest parts of parenting is finding out who our kids are. What makes them special and great? It's not always going to be the A honor roll and a throw like Manning's. Our kids are our gifts from God, but they're his creations. It might feel disappointing to realize they're not living up to your list of expectations (Lord knows God's thinkin' the same about me), but those differences can be amazing. It's really a lifelong adventure getting to know what makes our special ones tick, and if we just nurture them, and love them as they are, they'll surprise the heck out of us along the way, in a good way.

I used to be depressed about my son's lack of academic ambition and what seemed like general apathy toward life (dear God, *where* did I go wrong?!). He didn't like anything he tried—karate, music, sports, clubs, nothing. But then one day he discovered drawing, and the rest is history. When he showed me a sketch for the first time, he might as well have discovered an alternate energy source, I was so shocked. Not only because I was so devoid of any visual art skill myself, but because, shamefully, I had nearly given up on him. The guilt alone led me to buy that boy a state-of-the-art drawing desk within a week. Go. Create. Stop playing Xbox.

I remember my sister similarly spilling tears of disappointment for days after her ten-year-old quit the fiddle, simply because he didn't like it anymore. He had already fulfilled his end of the bargain by trying for one year before choosing whether to continue, but man, that was a harsh deal. I swear you could hear angels sing when those fingers fiddled.

Accepting, nurturing, and also being observant of your kids' learning and communication styles really make all the difference. I used to get so bent out of shape that my youngest resisted all things spiritual, like wanting to do morning devotionals, memorizing scripture, and praying aloud. I was practically breaking off generational curses, anointing his bed with oil, and racking my brain about how I'd hindered my three-year-old's spiritual growth.

But then, around four, he started busting out with epiphanies and profound biblical truths that caused my jaw to drop. "Don't worry, Mom. The Holy Spirit will lead you." "Mom, I know why

God made more than animals. He wanted to have someone to love, just like why people have kids." I realize now that Kenai was simply not a "joiner." He didn't like the feeling of forced, generic prayer, and repetitious scripture-touting … but he was absorbing and listening, despite what I mistook for his wayward soul shunning the light of Christ.

Our kids will surprise us, if we let them be who they are and love every weird, unpredictable part of them. Just because they're not where we'd hoped they'd be now doesn't mean they won't even exceed our expectations later on. A comforting thought when your six-year-old tells you he wants to be a disco DJ someday. "We'll pray on that, sweetie." Here's a trombone.

CHAPTER 36

Six Things We Learn about God through Having Kids

Having kids gives us such a special, powerful glimpse into so many of God's characteristics I'm not sure we'd fully grasp without becoming parents. For one, I don't know if I truly understood (will we ever?) the capacity of God's unconditional love until having children. So many of us tend to think we have to earn our way into God's favor and grace, especially after sinning, *again*, or not "performing" the way we should. If God loves us even more than earthly parents love their kids, as his Word states, then having kids obliterates these false beliefs of his love coming with strings attached.

Most mothers, Christian or not, love their kids no matter what. Period. We've all seen the mother of some serial killer pleading for the life of her convicted son because she'll always, always see him as her baby, despite his egregious acts. I get it, to a much lesser degree. I thought my maternal feelings might never return after my son deleted a most valuable, ever-so-long work project. But it's impossible not to forgive and love them unconditionally. It forces us to see ourselves in the same light. God loves us even more than we love our kids, through our ugly attitudes, rebellious times, and unappreciative seasons. I wonder how much more freedom and power we'd have in our lives if we really embraced that truth. I still don't know what to say about 2007–08, Lord, but thank you for your faithfulness.

He Has No Favorites

I have jealous tendencies. Started in second grade when my crush gave his hall pass to an undeserving blonde, who I'm sure *purposely* rolled up her uniform skirt, and it's been a thorn in my side to this day. So until I had kids I always had a hard time understanding how God could be completely devoted and equally in love with every single one of us. Millions roaming the earth, Lord, and you're really caring about my prayers against varicose vein swelling? Surely you're more devoted to the lady over there, fasting for revival in Asia. But after you rebel against sanity and have multiple children, it's amazing how your heart simply just expands and you love the next with every ounce of wonder and adoration as your first. I know if by some unfortunate turn of events I followed the path of the Duggars, birthing sixteen more children, I'd love each the same. I've realized if a severely flawed un-mom almost completely devoid of patience feels this way, how much greater God's ability is to know and love each of his children, as if each were his favorite. There's a cool boldness and sweet confidence that enters your heart after really believing this.

God Wants Us to Be Happy

Almost everything we do is for our kids. We sacrifice our time, money, and for a season, sometimes our dreams to invest in their lives and make them happy. And we do it with joy (usually) because our delight *is* our kids. We love giving them gifts, seeing them get excited about life's simple joys, watching them experience new things, and seeing them succeed. Sometimes when I'm watching the kids laughing, playing, or peacefully sleeping, I picture what it must be like to be God, just delighting over us enjoying the world he's created. Whenever I doubt whether God's hearing my prayers, or whether to listen and trust him with my hopes and dreams, I think about my attitude and love toward my kids and remember how much greater his love is for us. He already gave it all for us, but he promises to give abundant life, if we trust him. I think a part of my heart never really "got" that, until feeling the power of love as a mother.

His Ways Are Higher

Somewhere between explaining to Kenai that it's not good to eat candle wax and that he'd meet Jesus early if he kept shoving toys into sockets, I thought, *This must be what God feels like.* He's always giving us continual warnings and noes, as we stare blank-eyed, nod, and then continue to exude our own will. After a near-full-body shock, I finally told Kenai he just had to trust Mommy on this one and avoid sockets altogether, regardless if he understood electrical current grids. And God asks the same thing of us sometimes, regardless if we understand or agree with what he's asking of us. When we hear "Avoid that relationship" or "Don't take that job," or just "Wait," it can be hard to trust and obey, but God always has our best interest in mind. I often think if we operated in the kind of childlike faith our kids exude toward us, we'd avoid oh so many mistakes and enjoy a lot more victories.

God Disciplines Those He Loves

One of the worst parts of parenting is seeing your kids disobey, sin, or make choices that you know they'll regret. Whether it's lying about schoolwork at age seven, or watching something they shouldn't at fifteen, it angers us, but saddens us even more, because we want them to form life-giving habits and character traits that'll keep them close to the Lord through life. So we punish, correct, and patiently work with them, never giving up or refusing to believe they'll get better. It's difficult when our kids veer off the right path, even temporarily, or misbehave in ways that surprise us; but those experiences have brought me closer to God, feeling grateful for the mercy and patience he's shown when I've fallen into sin or chosen to believe lies that have kept me from him. It makes me that much more grateful for his mercy and unfailing kindness, and really keeps me committed to patiently but firmly disciplining my kids. So. Much. Mercy.

When we learn to trust him, be content in the moment, and focus on the blessings we have, motherhood becomes more enjoyable, and much easier, in time. Just like our relationships and our walk with the Lord, it's a journey. We just have to love our kids through the questions, trials, and victories and know God will work everything for good.

And until then, there's always hiding in the prayer closet.

Afterword

The hope of my heart is that even one woman who's pregnant and questioning whether to keep her baby would stumble upon this book. If there's any message worth sharing, aside from the life-giving salvation Christ offers, it's that motherhood is the single greatest blessing on earth. I've been there. Having a child when you're not expecting it might be the scariest, most inconvenient, and most impossible-seeming concept, but it is always, always worth it. Nothing in this world is worth losing your child. God is so good. You are enough for your baby. God will give you the strength, guidance, and provision to make it as a mom, if you follow him and learn to trust in the one who's had a plan for your life since creation. Your baby is not a mistake, and there is nothing—no circumstance or "accident"—God won't make beautiful. If you're pregnant, this *is* your path. And he'll make it an amazing one.

Acknowledgments

A deeply felt thanks to a beautiful human being and brilliant agent, Tawny Johnson—your vision and commitment have made my greatest dream come true. I'd say you're the wind beneath my wings, but we're both far too sarcastic for such nonsense. I'd be nowhere without my amazing mother, June, and sisters, Jill and Jocelyn—you have truly been the backbone of my life, and I'm so grateful for your unfailing support and faith in me. Thank you, Ingrid Beck, for saying yes to a slightly unhinged rookie author, and to Alice Crider and the entire DC Cook team—it's an honor to join your mission of inspiring people in their faith. Thank you, Nicci Jordan Hubert—your editorial talent and dedication are rare. A special thanks to my soul sister, Lindsay, and Allison, Becky, Lucy, Uni, Arielle, Dianne, Terry, and Isa, and all the amazing women who've inspired and supported me through motherhood, and other near disasters. Thank you for the laughter, and never batting an eye when I run out of gas on the way to playgroup. And of course, my greatest thanks to God, for blessing me so much more than I deserve.

Join the #UnMom Community Page

Want to laugh out loud as you realize you're not alone in your #UnMom struggles?

Want to share you personal #UnMom stories with other #UnMoms?

Laugh, cry, and share your stories at
bit.ly/unmom-community